A BASIC MUSIC LIBRARY

ESSENTIAL SCORES AND BOOKS

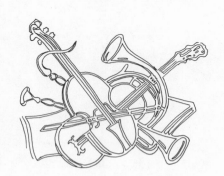

Compiled by the

MUSIC LIBRARY ASSOCIATION

SUBCOMMITTEE ON BASIC MUSIC COLLECTION

Edited by

PAULINE SHAW BAYNE

AMERICAN LIBRARY ASSOCIATION

Chicago 1978

Library of Congress Cataloging in Publication Data

Music Library Association. Subcommittee on Basic Music
    Collection.
    A basic music library.

    Includes index.
    1. Music--Bibliography. I. Bayne, Pauline Shaw.
II. Title.
ML113.M8845   016.78   78-11997
ISBN 0-8389-0281-2

Copyright © 1978 by the Music Library Association

Printed in the United States of America

TABLE OF CONTENTS

Preface   v

Study Scores
    Orchestral Music   1
    Chamber Music for Strings   13
    Chamber Music with Winds   25

Performing Editions
    Chamber Music for Strings   35
    Chamber Music with Winds   45
    Songs for Solo Voice with Piano
        or Orchestra   53

Piano-Vocal Scores
    Operas, Oratorios, etc.   63

Music Literature
    Reference Books   73
    Biographies   85
    American Music: Books   95
    Periodicals and Yearbooks   105

Methods
    Instrumental Methods and Studies   117

Music Publishers: Their Addresses and
    American Agents   137

Index   141

PREFACE

A Basic Music Library: Essential Scores and Books
is a series of select lists of music and books about
music prepared to assist small and medium-sized general
libraries in enriching their music collections. With
the growing interest in music, no library, however small,
should be without a basic collection of music and music
reference sources. Every community has a number of amateur and professional musicians who need the services of
a good music collection, and it is hoped that this publication will aid libraries in meeting this need.

Libraries generally maintain a sizeable record
collection. This series of lists is also intended to
complement and, whenever possible, closely relate to a
basic record collection. A Basic Record Library, distri-
buted by Schwann Record and Tape Guide at a cost of
$.75, serves as a guide to such a record collection. It
is readily available and is not restricted to specific
recorded performances.

The twelve lists included here contain citations
for books and scores which were in print and available
at the quoted prices in January 1978. Scores are
generally issued in paperbound editions; therefore, any
clothbound editions are so indicated. For books cloth-
bound editions are to be assumed unless paperback publications are so specified. The total price for each
list is figured in terms of the least expensive editions
listed; thus, the total cost of a list is a minimum
according to prices in January 1978.

Whenever a list is arranged according to composer,
the composers' names and dates are given as they appear
on Library of Congress cards. For scores, the bracketed
title is the uniform (filing) title, following Library
of Congress practice and the Anglo-American Cataloging

<u>Rules</u>. The second title given for scores is generally
the heading under which that work will be found in the
monthly issues of the <u>Schwann Record and Tape Guide</u> or
its semi-annual supplement, <u>Schwann-2</u>. Frequently,
several publishers have been cited for a single score
title; however, other editions of the work may also be
available. The scores may be supplied by any reputable
music dealer. Order by composer, title, contents (if
not specified by the uniform title), and such format
terms as "study score," "piano-vocal score," or "performing parts."

Many of the lists contain more works than a small
library could purchase; for this reason, some of the
more essential items have been identified in such cate-
gories as Reference Books and Periodicals. It is
assumed that librarians will make choices according to
the needs of their particular clientele.

<u>A Basic Music Library: Essential Scores and Books</u>
does not yet cover all music subject areas that should
be included in a music collection of books and scores,
but the compilation will be reissued periodically to up-
date the existing lists and to provide additional lists
of materials in other music areas. The Music Library
Association hopes that greater distribution of the lists
will be possible in this collective, monographic form so
that they may better serve the purpose of assisting
libraries which do not have music specialists.

Many people have contributed to this Music Library
Association project over the years, and it is appropriate
that these individuals be given credit for their work.
The lists were originally designed and published as
individual pamphlets to be used as buying guides and
tools for collection evaluation by librarians in public,
college, and smaller university libraries. Walter
Gerboth and James Pruett were among the prime movers
of the basic list concept. A number of committees have
prepared these lists.

The first four lists (Reference Books; Study Scores:
Orchestral Music; Biographies; and Vocal Music: Operas,
Oratorios, etc.), published in 1970, were prepared from
original compilations by members of the M.L.A. Selection
and Acquisition Committee: Ethel Bacon, Mattie Barclay,
John F. Bundy, Emanuel Dondy, Carol Walden, and
Franklin P. Taplin, chairperson.

Published in 1974, lists 5-8 (Study Scores: Chamber
Music for Strings; Performing Editions: Chamber Music

for Strings; Study Scores: Chamber Music with Winds;
and Performing Editions: Chamber Music with Winds) were
the work of the 1973 M.L.A. Selection and Acquisition
Committee: Robert Jones, Ida Reed, Jean Geil, and
Katherine Holum, chairperson. List 9, American Music:
Books, was prepared for the Music Library Association
by associates of the Institute for Studies in American
Music of Brooklyn College, H. Wiley Hitchcock, director.
The compilers were Angelo Corbo, Jack Justice, Robin
Warren, and Judith Tick with the assistance of Walter
Gerboth, chairperson.

Late in 1973 the Subcommittee on Basic Music
Collection was formed with the sole purpose of revising
existing lists and preparing new ones for publication.
The subcommittee members from 1973 to 1975 were Robert
Daw, J. Michael Foster, Pauline Shaw, and Dorothy
McAdoo Bognar, chairperson. This subcommittee worked
on the publication of lists 5-8 which had been prepared
earlier.

From 1975 to 1978 the members of the group were
Phyllis Anderson (1975-1977), Carole Franklin, Stephen
Fry, William C. Rorick (1977-1978), Nyal Williams, and
Pauline Shaw Bayne, chairperson. The subcommittee
worked from original compilations by its members:
Periodicals and Yearbooks by Nyal Williams, Instrumental
Methods and Studies by William C. Rorick, Songs for Solo
Voice and Piano by Carole Franklin, and a new list of
Reference Books by Stephen Fry. Revision of the lists
of American Music: Books and Biographies, as well as
the price and availability information for all of the
score lists, and final decisions on all inclusions were
the responsibilities of Pauline Shaw Bayne.

We of the 1978 Subcommittee on Basic Music Collection would like to thank the members of the M.L.A.
Publications Committee, chaired by John W. Tanno, with
particular thanks to Lenore Coral and Linda Solow
for their editorial assistance during the preparation
of the lists for this monograph and for the final preparation of the manuscript.

Pauline Shaw Bayne, Chairperson
M.L.A. Subcommittee on Basic
Music Collection

February 1978

S T U D Y   S C O R E S:
O R C H E S T R A L   M U S I C

A study score is a relatively inexpensive score, usually paperbound and with the musical notation photographically reduced in size, which is more suitable for following than for performing music. This list of study scores, which are also called miniature or pocket scores, includes only orchestral music and is designed to further the use of such scores. At the time of compilation, the approximate cost of the entire list was $375.00.

BACH, Johann Sebastian, 1685-1750.
1. [Concerti grossi] Brandenburg Concerti (6), S.1046/51. Boosey & Hawkes: issued separately, $3.75 each; $22.50 total. Eulenburg: issued separately, $3.25; $19.50 total. Kalmus: 2v., $1.50 each; $3.00 total. Lea: 2v., $1.75 each; $3.50 total.

2. [Concerto, harpsichord & string orchestra, S.1052, D minor] Concerti (7) for Harpsichord . . . No. 1 in d, S.1052. Boosey & Hawkes: $3.00. Eulenburg: $3.75. Kalmus: 2v., nos. 1-7 (all), $2.00 each; $4.00 total. Lea: nos. 1 & 2, $1.75.

3. [Concerto, violin & string orchestra, S.1041, A minor] Concerti (2) for Violin. Boosey & Hawkes: $5.00. Kalmus: $2.00. Lea: with Concerto, violin, S.1042, $1.75.

4. [Concerto, violin & string orchestra, S.1042, E major] Concerti (2) for Violin. Boosey & Hawkes: $3.00. Kalmus: with Concerto, Violin, S.1041, $2.00. Lea: with Concerto, Violin, S.1041, $1.75.

5. [Suites, orchestra, S.1066-1069] Suites (4) for
    orchestra, S.1066/9. Eulenburg: issued
    separately, $3.25 each; $13.00 total. Lea: $1.75.

BARTÓK, Béla, 1881-1945.
6. [Concerto, orchestra] Concerto for Orchestra
    (1943). Boosey & Hawkes: $11.00.

7. [Music, celesta, percussion & string orchestra]
    Music for Strings, Percussion, Celesta (1935).
    Boosey & Hawkes: $13.00. Philharmonia: $8.50.

BEETHOVEN, Ludwig van, 1770-1827.
8. [Concerto, piano, no. 3, op. 37, C minor] Con-
    certi (5) for Piano & Orchestra, No. 3 in c,
    Op. 37. Boosey & Hawkes: $5.00. Eulenburg:
    $5.00. Kalmus: nos. 3-5, $4.00.

9. [Concerto, piano, no. 4, op. 58, G major] Con-
    certi (5) for Piano & Orchestra, No. 4 in G,
    Op. 58. Boosey & Hawkes: $5.00. Eulenburg:
    $5.00. Kalmus: nos. 3-5, $4.00. Philharmonia:
    $3.75.

10. [Concerto, piano, no. 5, op. 73, E flat major]
    Concerti (5) for Piano & Orchestra, No. 5 in E
    flat, Op. 73. Boosey & Hawkes: $5.00. Eulen-
    burg: $5.00. Kalmus: nos. 3-5, $4.00.

11. [Concerto, violin, op. 61, D major] Concerto
    in D for Violin, Op. 61. Boosey & Hawkes:
    $5.00. Eulenburg: $3.75. Kalmus: $2.50. Phil-
    harmonia: $2.75.

12. [Coriolan overture] Overtures. Boosey & Hawkes:
    $3.50. Eulenburg: $3.25. Kalmus: $4.25.

13. [Egmont. Overture] Overtures. Boosey & Hawkes:
    $5.00. Eulenburg: $3.25. Kalmus: $4.25. Phil-
    harmonia: $2.25.

14. Leonore overture, no. 3] Overtures. Boosey &
    Hawkes: $3.75. Eulenburg: $3.25. Kalmus: $4.25.
    Philharmonia: $2.25.

15. [Symphony, no. 3, op. 55, E flat major] Sym-
     phonies . . . No. 3 in E flat, Op. 55. Boosey
     & Hawkes: $6.00. Eulenburg: $4.50. Kalmus:
     nos. 1-4, $4.50. Philharmonia: $3.25.

16. [Symphony, no. 5, op. 67, C minor] Symphonies
     . . . No. 5 in c, Op. 67. Boosey & Hawkes:
     $2.75. Eulenburg: $4.50. Kalmus: nos. 5-7,
     $4.50. Philharmonia: $3.25.

17. [Symphony, no. 6, op. 68, F major] Symphonies
     . . . No. 6 in F, Op. 68. Boosey & Hawkes:
     $5.00. Eulenburg: $4.50. Kalmus: nos. 5-7,
     $4.50. Philharmonia: $3.25.

18. [Symphony, no. 9, op. 125, D minor] Symphonies
     . . . No. 9 in d, Op. 125. Boosey & Hawkes:
     $12.00. Eulenburg: $6.00. Kalmus: nos. 8-9,
     $4.50. Philharmonia: $4.75.

BERG, Alban, 1885-1935.
   19. [Concerto, violin] Concerto for Violin and
        Orchestra (1935). Philharmonia: $8.00.

BERLIOZ, Hector, 1803-1869.
   20. [Symphonie fantastique] Symphonie fantastique,
        Op. 14. Eulenburg: $4.00. Kalmus: $4.00.

BORODIN, Aleksandr Porfir'evich, 1833-1887.
   21. [Kniaz' Igor'. Polovet͡skai͡a plĭaska] Prince
        Igor: Polovetsian Dances. Eulenburg: $.75.
        Kalmus: $4.00

BRAHMS, Johannes, 1833-1897.
   22. [Akademische Festouverture] Academic Festival
        Overture, Op. 80. Boosey & Hawkes: $3.75.
        Eulenburg: $3.25. Kalmus: $1.50.

   23. [Concerto, piano, no. 1, op. 15, D minor] Con-
        certo No. 1 in d for Piano, Op. 15. Eulenburg:
        $6.00. Kalmus: $4.00.

   24. [Concerto, piano, no. 2, op. 83, B flat major]
        Concerto No. 2 in B flat for Piano, Op. 83.
        Boosey & Hawkes: $3.50. Eulenburg: $7.00.
        Kalmus: $5.00.

25.   [Concerto, violin, op. 77, D major]   Concerto
      in D for Violin, Op. 77. Eulenburg: $5.50.
      Kalmus: $3.50.

26.   [Symphony, no. 1, op. 68, C minor] Symphonies
      . . . No. 1 in c, Op. 68. Boosey & Hawkes:
      $6.50. Eulenburg: $5.50. Kalmus: nos. 1-2,
      $4.00. Philharmonia, $4.25.

27.   [Symphony, no. 4, op. 98, E minor] Symphonies
      . . . No. 4 in e, Op. 98. Boosey & Hawkes:
      $6.50. Eulenburg: $5.50. Kalmus: nos. 3-4,
      $4.00. Philharmonia: $4.25.

28.   [Variationen über ein Thema von Haydn, orchestra]
      Variations on a Theme by Haydn, Op. 56a. Boosey
      & Hawkes: $3.75. Eulenburg: $3.25. Kalmus:
      $3.50.

BRITTEN, Benjamin, 1913-
29.   [The Young person's guide to the orchestra]
      Young Person's Guide to the Orchestra, Op. 34
      (1946). Boosey & Hawkes: $7.50.

CHAĬKOVSKIĬ, Petr Il'ich, 1840-1893.
30.   [Concerto, piano, no. 1, op. 23, B flat minor]
      Concerto No. 1 in b flat for Piano & Orchestra,
      Op. 23. Boosey & Hawkes: $3.00. Eulenburg:
      $6.00. Kalmus: $4.00.

31.   [The Nutcracker. Suite] Nutcracker Suite, Op.
      71a. Eulenburg: $5.00. Kalmus: $3.50.

32.   [The Swan Lake. Selections] Swan Lake
      (excerpts). Boosey & Hawkes: $6.00. Eulenburg:
      $7.00. Kalmus: $3.50.

33.   [Symphony, no. 6, op. 74, B minor] Symphony
      No. 6 in b, Op. 74, "Pathetique." Boosey &
      Hawkes: $6.00. Eulenburg: $5.50. Kalmus:
      $5.00. Philharmonia: $4.25.

COPLAND, Aaron, 1900-
34.   [Appalachian spring (suite)] Appalachian Spring:
      Suite. Boosey & Hawkes: $9.50.

CORELLI, Arcangelo, 1653-1713.
    35. [Concerto grosso, op. 6, no. 8, G minor] Con-
        certo Grosso, Op. 6, No. 8, "Christmas."
        Eulenburg: $3.75. Kalmus: Op. 6, nos. 7-12,
        $1.50. Lea: Op. 6, nos. 7-12, $1.75.

DEBUSSY, Claude, 1862-1918.
    36. [La mer] La Mer (1903-5). Durand: $11.50.
        Eulenburg: $8.50. International: $6.00.

    37. [Prélude à l'après-midi d'un faune] Prélude à
        l'après-midi d'un faune (1892-4). Eulenburg:
        $3.75. International: $2.50. Kalmus: $1.75.

DUKAS, Paul Abraham, 1865-1935.
    38. [L'apprenti sorcier] Sorcerer's Apprentice
        (1897). Eulenburg: $4.00. International: $3.50.
        Kalmus: $4.00.

DVOŘÁK, Antonín, 1841-1904.
    39. [Symphony, no. 9, op. 95, E minor] Symphony No.
        9 in e, Op. 95, "New World" (old No. 5).
        Boosey & Hawkes: $3.00. Eulenburg: $6.00.
        Kalmus: $3.50.

FRANCK, César Auguste, 1822-1890.
    40. [Symphony, D minor] Symphony in d. Eulenburg:
        $5.00. Kalmus: $3.50.

GERSHWIN, George, 1898-1937.
    41. [Rhapsody in blue, piano & orchestra] Rhapsody
        in Blue (1924). Warner Brothers: $6.00.

GRIEG, Edvard Hagerup, 1843-1907.
    42. [Concerto, piano, op. 16, A minor] Concerto in
        a for Piano, Op. 16. Eulenburg: $6.00. Kalmus:
        $2.00.

    43. [Peer Gynt (Suite) no. 1] Peer Gynt Suites Nos.
        1 & 2, Op. 46, 55; or Peer Gynt Suite No. 1,
        Op. 46. Eulenburg: nos. 1-2, $5.50. Kalmus:
        no. 1, $3.50.

    44. [Peer Gynt (Suite) no. 2] Peer Gynt Suites Nos.
        1 & 2, Op. 46, 55. Eulenburg: nos. 1-2, $5.50.

HÄNDEL, Georg Friedrich, 1685-1759.
    45. [Fireworks music] <u>Royal Fireworks Music</u>.
        Boosey & Hawkes: $4.00. Eulenburg: $4.50.
        Lea: with <u>Water Music</u>, $1.75.

    46. [Water music] <u>Water Music</u> (complete). Boosey
        & Hawkes: $5.00. Eulenburg: $6.00. Lea: with
        <u>Fireworks Music</u>, $1.75.

HAYDN, Joseph, 1732-1809.
    47. [Symphony, M.45, F sharp minor] Symphony No.
        45 in f sharp, "Farewell." Eulenburg: $3.75.
        International $2.00. Kalmus: Symphony nos.
        44-46, $2.00. Philharmonia: $2.75.

    48. [Symphony, M.94, G major] Symphony No. 94 in
        G, "Surprise." Boosey & Hawkes: $3.75. Eulen-
        burg: $3.75. Kalmus: $2.00. Philharmonia: $3.25.

    49. [Symphony, M.101, D major] Symphony No. 101 in
        D, "Clock." Boosey & Hawkes: $3.75. Eulenburg:
        $3.75. Kalmus: $2.00. Philharmonia: $3.25.

    50. [Symphony, M.104, D major] Symphony No. 104 in
        D, "London." Boosey & Hawkes: $3.75. Eulenburg:
        $3.75. Kalmus: $2.00. Philharmonia: $3.25.

HINDEMITH, Paul, 1895-1963.
    51. [Mathis der Maler (Symphony)] <u>Mathis der Maler</u>
        (symphony) (1934). Schott: $7.50.

    52. [Symphonic metamorphosis of themes by Carl Maria
        Von Weber] <u>Symphonic Metamorphoses of Themes by</u>
        <u>Weber</u>. Schott: $7.00.

KODÁLY, Zoltán, 1882-1967.
    53. [Háry János. Suite] Háry János: Suite. Phil-
        harmonia: $8.50. Schott: $8.50.

LISZT, Franz, 1811-1886.
    54. [Concerto, piano, no. 1, E flat major] Con-
        certo No. 1 in E flat for Piano and Orchestra.
        Eulenburg: $5.50. Kalmus: $3.00.

    55. [Les preludes] <u>Les Preludes</u>, Symphonic Poem No.
        3. Eulenburg: $3.75. Kalmus: $2.50.

MAHLER, Gustave, 1860-1911.
  56.   [Lieder eines fahrenden Gesellen] Songs of a
        Wayfarer (1883). Eulenburg: $6.00. Kalmus:
        $3.00.

  57.   [Symphony, no. 2, C minor] Symphony No. 2 in
        c, "Resurrection." Kalmus: $6.00. Phil-
        harmonia: $13.95.

  58.   [Symphony, no. 4, G major] Symphony No. 4 in
        G (1900). Eulenburg: $10.00. Kalmus: $6.00.
        Philharmonia: $9.00.

MENDELSSOHN-BARTHOLDY, Felix, 1809-1847.
  59.   [Concerto, violin, op. 64, E minor] Concerto
        in e for Violin. Boosey & Hawkes: $6.00.
        Eulenburg: $5.00. Kalmus: $3.00.

  60.   [Ein Sommernachtstraum] Midsummer Night's Dream,
        Inc. Music, Op. 61. (NB: The Overture & Inci-
        dental Music appear together on the recordings
        listed under this heading; the scores of each
        opus are published separately). Eulenburg:
        $5.00. Kalmus: $6.00 (complete).

  61.   [Ein Sommernachtstraum. Overture] Midsummer
        Night's Dream, Inc. Music, Op. 21. (NB: The
        Overture & Incidental Music appear together on
        the recordings listed under this heading; the
        scores of each opus are published separately).
        Boosey & Hawkes: $3.75. Eulenburg: $3.25.
        Kalmus: $1.75. Philharmonia: $2.25.

  62.   [Symphony, no. 4, op. 90, A major] Symphony No.
        4 in A, Op. 90, "Italian." Boosey & Hawkes:
        $6.00. Eulenburg: $6.00. Kalmus: $4.50.

MOZART, Johann Chrysostom Wolfgang Amadeus, 1756-1791.
  63.   [Concerto, piano, K. 466, D minor] Concerti (25)
        for Piano & Orchestra, No. 20, in d, K. 466.
        Eulenburg: $5.50. Kalmus: $2.00.

  64.   [Concerto, piano, K. 488, A major] Concerti (25)
        for Piano & Orchestra, No. 23 in A, K. 488.
        Boosey & Hawkes: $6.00. Eulenburg: $5.50.
        Kalmus: $2.00. Philharmonia: $1.75.

65. [Eine kleine Nachtmusik] Serenade in G, K. 525,
     "Eine kleine Nachtmusik." Boosey & Hawkes: $2.75.
     Eulenburg: $2.25. Kalmus: $1.00. Lea: $1.75.
     Philharmonia: $1.25.

66. [Symphony, K. 504, D major] Symphonies (41),
     No. 38 in D, K. 504, "Prague." Boosey & Hawkes:
     $3.50. Eulenburg: $2.75. Kalmus: $2.00.
     Philharmonia: $1.75.

67. [Symphony, K. 550, G minor] Symphonies (41), No.
     40 in g, K. 550. Boosey & Hawkes: $4.00. Eulen-
     burg: $2.75. Kalmus: $2.00. Philharmonia: $1.75.

68. [Symphony, K. 551, C major] Symphonies (41), No.
     41 in C, K. 551, "Jupiter." Boosey & Hawkes:
     $4.25. Eulenburg: $2.75. Kalmus: $2.00.
     Philharmonia: $2.25.

MUSORGSKIĬ, Modest Petrovich, 1839-1881.
69. [Pictures at an exhibition; arr.] Pictures at
     an Exhibition. (NB: piano and orchestral re-
     corded versions are listed together; the original
     version is for piano.) Boosey & Hawkes: $8.75.
     Eulenburg: $8.75. Kalmus: $10.00 (piano version).

PROKOF'EV, Sergeĭ Sergeevich, 1891-1953.
70. [Classical symphony] Classical Symphony. Boo-
     sey & Hawkes: $11.00. Eulenburg: (Ed. Peters),
     $12.00. International: $3.00. Kalmus: $2.50.

71. [Peter and the wolf] Peter and the Wolf, Op. 67
     (1936). Boosey & Hawkes: $9.00. Eulenburg:
     $7.50. Kalmus: $3.00.

RACHMANINOFF, Sergei, 1873-1943.
72. [Concerto, piano, no. 2, op. 18, C minor] Con-
     certo No. 2 in c for Piano, Op. 18 (1901).
     Boosey & Hawkes: $15.00. Kalmus: $5.00.

73. [Rapsodie sur un thème de Paganini, piano and
     orchestra] Rhapsody on a Theme of Paganini,
     Op. 43 (1943). Belwin Mills: $6.00.

RAVEL, Maurice, 1875-1937.
74. [Bolero, orchestra] Bolero (1927). Durand:
    $10.50.

75. [Daphnis et Chloe. Suite no. 2] Daphnis et
    Chloe: Suite No. 2. Durand: $10.00.

RIMSKIĬ-KORSAKOV, Nikolaĭ Andreevich, 1844-1908.
76. [Scheherazade] Scheherazade, Op. 35. Eulen-
    burg: $8.50. Kalmus: $5.00.

ROSSINI, Gioacchino Antonio, 1792-1868.
77. [Il barbiere di Siviglia. Overture] Overtures.
    Eulenburg: $3.25. Kalmus: $2.00. Philharmonia:
    $2.25.

78. [Guillaume Tell. Overture] Overtures. Eulen-
    burg: $3.75. Kalmus: $2.50.

SCHÖNBERG, Arnold, 1784-1951.
79. [Verklärte Nacht] Verklärte Nacht, Op. 4
    (1899). International: $3.00. Kalmus: $2.00.

SCHUBERT, Franz Peter, 1797-1828.
80. [Symphony, D. 759, B minor] Symphony No. 8 in
    b, "Unfinished," Boosey & Hawkes: $1.50.
    Eulenburg: $3.25. Kalmus: $2.00. Philharmonia:
    $2.25.

SCHUMANN, Robert Alexander, 1810-1856.
81. [Concerto, piano, op. 54, A minor] Concerto in
    a for Piano & Orchestra, Op. 54. Boosey &
    Hawkes: $15.00. Eulenburg: $5.00. Kalmus:
    $2.00. Philharmonia: $3.75.

82. [Symphony, no. 3, op. 97, E flat major] Sym-
    phonies . . . No. 3 in E flat, Op. 97, "Rhenish."
    Eulenburg: $6.00. Kalmus: nos. 1-4 (all),
    $5.00. Philharmonia: $4.00.

SHOSTAKOVICH, Dmitriĭ Dmitrievich, 1906-
83. [Symphony, no. 5, op. 47] Symphony No. 5, Op.
    47 (1937). Eulenburg: $8.50. Kalmus: $6.00.

SIBELIUS, Jean, 1865-1957.
   84. [Finlandia] <u>Finlandia</u>, Op. 26 (1899). Kalmus:
       $1.00.

   85. [Symphony, no. 2, op. 43, D major] Symphonies
       . . . No. 2 in D, Op. 43 (1901). Kalmus: $3.50.

SMETANA, Bedřich, 1824-1884.
   86. [Má vlast, Vltava] Moldau (Vltava) (from: <u>My</u>
       <u>Fatherland</u>). Boosey & Hawkes: $2.75. Eulen-
       burg: $5.00. Kalmus: $2.50.

STRAUSS, Johann, 1825-1899.
   87. [An der schönen Blauen Donau] Waltzes (<u>The Blue</u>
       <u>Danube</u>). Eulenburg: $3.75. Kalmus: $2.00.

   88. [Geschichte aus dem Wiener Wald] Waltzes (<u>Tales</u>
       <u>from the Vienna Woods</u>). Kalmus: $2.00.

   89. [Kaiser-Walzer, orchestra] Waltzes (<u>Emperor</u>
       <u>Waltz</u>). Eulenburg: $3.75. Kalmus: $2.00.

STRAUSS, Richard, 1864-1949.
   90. [Don Juan] <u>Don Juan</u>, Op. 20 (1888). Eulenburg:
       $6.00. Kalmus: $4.00.

   91. [Till Eulenspiegels lustige Streiche] <u>Till</u>
       <u>Eulenspiegel</u>, Op. 28 (1895). Eulenburg: $5.50.
       Kalmus: $4.00.

STRAVINSKIĬ, Igor' Fedorovich, 1882-
   92. [L'oiseau de feu. Suite] <u>Firebird Suite</u>. (NB:
       the 1919 edition). Boosey & Hawkes: $7.50.
       Eulenburg: $9.00. Kalmus: $4.00.

   93. [Petroushka] <u>Petrouchka</u> (complete ballet) (1911).
       Boosey & Hawkes: $13.00. Kalmus: $4.00.

   94. [Le sacre du printemps] <u>Sacre du printemps</u>
       (1913). Boosey & Hawkes: $15.00. Kalmus: $4.00.

TCHAIKOVSKY <u>see</u> Chaĭkovskiĭ, Petr Il'ich

VILLA-LOBOS, Heitor, 1887-1959.
   95. [Bachianas brasilieras, no. 5, soprano & string
       orchestra] <u>Bachianas No. 5</u> for Soprano & 8

Celli (1938-45). Associated Music Publishers:
$2.50. Eulenburg: $5.00.

WEBER, Karl Maria Friedrich Ernst, Freiherr von, 1786-1826.
  96. [Der Freischutz. Overture] Overtures. Boosey
       & Hawkes: $2.75. Eulenburg: $3.25. Phil-
       harmonia: $2.25.

STUDY SCORES:
CHAMBER MUSIC FOR STRINGS

    This list includes chamber music since 1750 for
three to eight stringed instruments, with or without
piano accompaniment. At the time of compilation, the
approximate cost of the entire list was $315.00
exclusive of the collective editions listed under
section H. The collective editions total $38.50.

STRING TRIOS (violin, viola, violoncello)

BEETHOVEN, Ludwig van, 1770-1827.
    97.   [Trios, strings] Trios (strings) (5)(complete).
           Eulenburg: issued separately, $3.25 each; $9.75
           total. Lea: $1.75. Kalmus: $2.00.

MOZART, Johann Chrysostom Wolfgang Amadeus, 1756-1791.
    98.   [Divertimento, string trio, K.563, E flat
           major] Divertimento in E flat for String Trio,
           K. 563. Eulenburg: $3.25. International:
           $1.50.

SCHÖNBERG, Arnold, 1874-1951.
    99.   [Trio, strings, op. 45] Trio (string), Op. 45
           (1946). Bomart Music Publications: $4.00.

PIANO TRIOS (violin, violoncello, piano)

BEETHOVEN, Ludwig van, 1770-1827.
    100.   [Trios, piano & strings] Trios (piano) (9)
           (complete), Trio in B flat, Op. 11; Trio in G,
           Op. 121a (Kakadu): Variations in E flat, Op. 44.
           Kalmus: 3v., $2.00 each; $6.00 total. Lea: 3v.,
           $1.75 each; $5.25 total.

BRAHMS, Johannes, 1833-1897.
  101. [Trios, piano & strings] Trios (3) (piano)
        (complete). Eulenburg: issued separately,
        $3.75 each; $11.25 total. Kalmus: 2v., $2.00
        each; $4.00 total.

DVOŘÁK, Antonín, 1841-1904.
  102. [Trio, piano & strings, no. 4, op. 90, E minor]
        Trio in e, Op. 90, "Dumky." Eulenburg: $3.75.
        Lea: $4.25.

HAYDN, Joseph, 1732-1809.
  103. [Trios, piano & strings] Trios (piano) (31).
        Lea: 4v., $1.75 each; $7.00 total.

MENDELSSOHN-BARTHOLDY, Felix, 1809-1847.
  104. [Trios, piano & strings] Trio No. 1 in d (piano),
        Op. 49; Trio No. 2 in c (piano), Op. 66.
        Eulenburg: issued separately, $3.25 each;
        $6.50 total. Kalmus: $2.00.

MOZART, Johann Chrysostom Wolfgang Amadeus, 1756-1791.
  105. [Trios, piano & strings] Trios (piano) (7), K.
        254, 442, 496, 502, 542, 548, 564; includes also
        Trio in E flat for Clarinet, Viola, Piano, K.
        498. Kalmus: 2v., $2.00 each; $4.00 total.
        Lea: 2v., $1.75 each; $3.50 total.

RAVEL, Maurice, 1875-1937.
  106. [Trio, piano & strings, A minor] Trio in a
        (piano) (1914). Durand: $6.00.

SCHUBERT, Franz Peter, 1797-1828.
  107. [Trios, piano & strings] Trio No. 1 in B flat
        (piano), Op. 99, D. 898; Trio No. 2 in E flat
        (piano), Op. 100, D. 929; Nocturne in E flat,
        Op. 148, D. 897. Eulenburg: 3v., $3.25 each;
        $9.75 total. Kalmus: 2v., $2.00 each; $4.00
        total. Lea: $1.75.

SCHUMANN, Robert Alexander, 1810-1856.
  108. [Trios, piano & strings] Trios (3) for Violin,
        Cello, Piano, Op. 63, 80, 110. Eulenburg:
        issued separately, $3.25 each, $9.75 total.
        Kalmus: 2v., $2.00 each; $4.00 total.

SHOSTAKOVICH, Dmitriĭ Dmitrievich, 1906-   .
  109.   [Trio, piano & strings, no. 2, op. 67, E minor]
         Trio No. 2 in e (piano), Op. 67 (1944). Phil-
         harmonia: $2.95.

SMETANA, Bedřich, 1824-1884.
  110.   [Trio, piano & strings, op. 15, G minor]   Trio
         in g (piano), Op. 15. Eulenburg: $4.50.

STRING QUARTETS (2 violins, viola, violoncello)

BARTÓK, Béla, 1881-1945.
  111.   [Quartets, strings] Quartets (6) (complete).
         Boosey & Hawkes: $27.00, bound.

BEETHOVEN, Ludwig van, 1770-1827.
  112.   [Quartets, strings] Quartets (16) (complete).
         Boosey & Hawkes: issued separately, $1.25 each
         (Op. 18, nos. 1-6; Op. 59, no. 2; Op. 74; Op.
         127; Op. 130; Op. 132; Op. 133; Op. 135);
         $16.25 total. Eulenburg: issued separately,
         $2.75 each; $44.00 total. Kalmus: 4v., $1.50
         each; $6.00 total. Lea: 4v., $1.75 each; $7.00
         total. Philharmonia: issued separately,
         variously priced, $30.25 total.

BERG, Alban, 1885-1935.
  113.   [Lyrische Suite, string quartet] Lyric Suite
         for String Quartet (1926). Philharmonia: $7.00.

  114.   [Quartet, strings, op. 3] Quartet, Op. 3 (1910).
         Philharmonia: $4.25.

BORODIN, Aleksandr Porfir'evich, 1833-1887.
  115.   [Quartet, strings, no. 2, D major]   Quartet No.
         2 in D. Eulenburg: $3.75. International:
         $2.00.

BRAHMS, Johannes, 1833-1897.
  116.   [Quartets, strings] Quartets (3) (complete).
         Boosey & Hawkes: issued separately, Quartets
         Nos. 1 & 2, $2.25 each; $4.50 total. Phil-
         harmonia: 3v., $2.25 each; $6.75 total.

CARTER, Elliott Cook, 1908-
  117. [Quartet, strings, no. 1] Quartet (1951).
        Associated Music Publishers: $4.50.

  118. [Quartet, strings, no. 2] Quartet (1959).
        Associated Music Publishers: $4.00.

DEBUSSY, Claude, 1862-1918.
  119. [Quartet, strings, op. 10, G minor] Quartet
        in g, Op. 10 (1893). International: $2.50.
        Kalmus: $2.25.

DVOŘÁK, Antonín, 1841-1904.
  120. [Quartet, strings, B. 75, D minor] Quartet
        No. 2 in d, Op. 34. Boosey & Hawkes: $3.00.
        Lea: $4.00.

  121. [Quartet, strings, B. 92, E flat major] Quar-
        tet No. 3 in E flat, Op. 51. Boosey & Hawkes:
        $2.50. Lea: $4.00.

  122. [Quartet, strings, B. 121, C major] Quartet
        No. 4 in C, Op. 61. Boosey & Hawkes: $3.50.
        Lea: $4.00.

  123. [Quartet, strings, B. 179, F major] Quartet
        No. 6 in F, Op. 96, "American." Boosey &
        Hawkes: $3.00. International: $2.00. Kalmus:
        $1.50. Lea: $4.00.

  124. [Quartet, strings, B. 192, G major] Quartet
        No. 8 in G, Op. 106. Boosey & Hawkes: $2.00.
        Lea: $4.00.

  125. [Quartet, strings, B. 193, A flat major] Quar-
        tet No. 7 in A flat, Op. 105. Boosey & Hawkes:
        $3.00. Lea: $4.00.

HAYDN, Joseph, 1732-1809.
  126. [Quartets, strings. Selections] Quartets,
        Op. 3, Nos. 3, 5; Op. 9, No. 2; Op. 17, No. 5;
        Op. 20, Nos. 4-6; Op. 33, Nos. 2-3; Op. 33, No.
        6; Op. 54, Nos. 1-3; Op. 64, Nos. 2-6; Op. 74,
        Nos. 1-3, Op. 76, Nos. 1-6; Op. 77, Nos. 1-2.
        Eulenburg: issued separately, $2.50-$3.25 each;
        $93.00 total. Kalmus: 3v., $5.00 each; $15.00

total. Philharmonia: 10 quartets available,
issued separately, $1.75 each; $17.50 total.

HINDEMITH, Paul, 1895-1963.
  127. [Quartet, strings, op. 22] Quartet, Op. 22
        (1922). Schott: $3.75.

IVES, Charles Edward, 1874-1954.
  128. [Quartet, strings, no. 1] Quartet No. 1 (1896).
        Peer: $4.00.

  129. [Quartet, strings, no. 2] Quartet No. 2 (1913).
        Peer: $4.00.

JANÁČEK, Leoš, 1854-1928.
  130. [Quartet, strings, no. 2] Quartet No. 2 (1923).
        Boosey & Hawkes: $2.50.

LUTOSLAWSKI, Witold, 1913-
  131. [Quartet, strings] Quartet. Chester: $29.00.

MENDELSSOHN-BARTHOLDY, Felix, 1809-1847.
  132. [Quartets, strings] Quartets (7), Op. 12, 13,
        44, 44a, 44b, 80, 81. Kalmus: 2v., $2.00 each;
        $4.00 total. Lea: 2v., $1.75 each; $3.50 total.

MOZART, Johann Chrysostom Wolfgang Amadeus, 1756-1791.
  133. [Eine kleine Nachtmusik] Serenade in G, K. 525,
        "Eine kleine Nachtmusik." Boosey & Hawkes:
        $2.75. Eulenburg: $2.25. Lea: $1.75. Phil-
        harmonia: $1.25.

  134. [Quartets, strings. Selections] Quartets Nos.
        14-19, "Haydn Quartets;" No. 20 in D, K. 499;
        No. 21 in D, K. 575; No. 22 in B flat, K. 589;
        No. 23 in F, K. 590. Boosey & Hawkes: issued
        separately, $3.00 each; $18.00 total. Kalmus:
        2v., $2.00 each; $4.00 total. Philharmonia:
        issued separately, $1.75 each; $17.50 total.

NIELSEN, Carl, 1865-1931.
  135. [Quartet, strings, no. 4, op. 44, F major]
        Quartet, Op. 44. Eulenburg: $5.50.

PENDERECKI, Krzysztof, 1933-
  136. [Quartet, strings, no. 1] Quartet (1960). Ars
        Polana (i.e., PWM Poland): $3.00.

PROKOF'EV, Sergeĭ Sergeevich, 1891-1953.
  137.   [Quartet, strings, no. 1, op. 50]   Quartet No.
         1, Op. 50 (1931). Boosey & Hawkes: $4.50.
         International: $2.50.

  138.   [Quartet, strings, no. 2, op. 92]   Quartet No.
         2, Op. 92 (1941). International: $2.50.

RAVEL, Maurice, 1875-1937.
  139.   [Quartet, strings, F major]   Quartet in F
         (1902-03). International: $2.50.

SCHÖNBERG, Arnold, 1874-1951.
  140.   [Quartet, strings, no. 1, op. 7, D minor]
         Quartet No. 1 in d, Op. 7 (1904-05). Kalmus:
         $2.00. Universal: $7.50.

  141.   [Quartet, strings, no. 2, op. 10, F sharp
         minor] Quartet No. 2 in f sharp, Strings &
         Soprano, Op. 10 (1907-08). Philharmonia: $6.25.

  142.   [Quartet, strings, no. 3, op. 30] Quartet No.
         3, Op. 30 (1926). Philharmonia: $7.50.

  143.   [Quartet, strings, no. 4, op. 37] Quartet No.
         4, Op. 37 (1936). G. Schirmer: $3.50.

SCHUBERT, Franz, 1797-1828.
  144.   [Quartets, strings] Quartets (complete). Kal-
         mus: 3v., $1.50 each; $4.50 total. Lea: 3v.,
         $1.75 each; $5.25 total.

SCHUMANN, Robert, 1810-1856.
  145.   [Quartets, strings] Quartets (3), Op. 41 (com-
         plete). Eulenburg: issued separately, $3.25
         each; $9.75 total. Kalmus: $2.00. Phil-
         harmonia: issued separately, $2.25 each; $6.75
         total.

SHOSTAKOVICH, Dmitriĭ Dmitrievich, 1906-
  146.   [Quartet, strings, no. 1, E minor] Quartet No.
         8, Op. 110 (1962). Eulenburg: $5.00. Kalmus:
         2v., $3.00 each; $6.00 total.

SMETANA, Bedřich, 1824-1884.
147. [Quartet, strings, no. 1, E minor] Quartet
No. 1 in e, "From my Life." Boosey & Hawkes:
$2.35. Eulenburg: $3.25.

STRAVINSKIĬ, Igor' Fedorovich, 1882-1971.
148. [Concertino, string quartet] Concertino for
String Quartet (1920). Boosey & Hawkes: $3.75.
W. Hansen: $9.75.

149. [Pieces, string quartet] 3 Pieces for String
Quartet (1914). Boosey & Hawkes: $4.00.

WEBERN, Anton von, 1883-1945.
150. [Bagatelles, string quartet, op. 9] Six Bagatelles for String Quartet, Op. 9 (1913). Philharmonia: $2.75.

151. [Langsamer Satz, string quartet] Slow Movement,
for Quartet (1905). Boosey & Hawkes: $2.85.
Carl Fischer: $2.00.

152. [Quartet, strings (1905)] Quartet (1905).
Boosey & Hawkes: $3.30. Carl Fischer: $5.00.

153. [Quartet, strings, op. 28] Quartet, Op. 28
(1938). Philharmonia: $3.75.

154. [Sätze, string quartet, op. 5] Five Movements
for String Quartet, Op. 5 (1909). Philharmonia:
$3.25.

PIANO QUARTETS (violin, viola, violoncello, piano)

BRAHMS, Johannes, 1833-1897.
155. [Quartets, piano & strings] Quartets (3) for
Piano and Strings (complete). Eulenburg:
issued separately, $4.50 each; $13.50 total.
Kalmus: issued separately, $2.00 each; $6.00
total.

MOZART, Johann Chrysostom Wolfgang Amadeus, 1756-1791.
156. [Quartets, piano & strings] Quartets (piano)
in g, K. 478; in E flat, K. 493. Eulenburg:
issued separately, $3.25 each; $6.50 total.
Kalmus: $2.00. Lea: $1.75.

SCHUMANN, Robert Alexander, 1810-1856.
  157. [Quartet, piano & strings, op. 47, E flat major]
        Quartet in E flat for Piano & Strings, Op. 47.
        Eulenburg: $4.50. Kalmus: with his piano quar-
        tet, op. 44, $2.00.

STRING QUINTETS

BEETHOVEN, Ludwig van, 1770-1827.
  158. [Quintet, violins, violas & violoncello, op.
        29, C major] Quintet in C, Op. 29. Eulenburg:
        $3.75. Kalmus: $2.00. Lea: $1.75.

BRAHMS, Johannes, 1833-1897.
  159. [Quintet, violins, violas & violoncello, no. 1,
        op. 88, F major] Quintet No. 1 in F, Op. 88.
        Eulenburg: $3.25. Kalmus: $2.00.

  160. [Quintet, violins, violas & violoncello, no. 2,
        op. 111, G major] Quintet No. 2 in G, Op. 111.
        Eulenburg: $3.75. Kalmus: $2.00.

DVOŘÁK, Antonín, 1841-1904.
  161. [Quintet, violins, violas & violoncello, op.
        97, E flat major] Quintet No. 3 in E flat,
        Op. 97 (strings). Boosey & Hawkes: $3.25.
        Eulenburg: $4.50.

  162. [Quintet, violins, viola, violoncello & double
        bass, op. 77, G major] Quintet in G, Op. 77
        (orig. Op. 18). Boosey & Hawkes: $2.00. Eulen-
        burg: $4.50.

MOZART, Johann Chrysostom Wolfgang Amadeus, 1756-1791.
  163. [Quintets, violins, violas & violoncello]
        Quintets (6) K. 174, 406, 515, 516, 593, 614;
        includes also Quintet in E flat for Horn and
        Strings, K. 407. Kalmus: 2v., $2.00 each; $4.00
        total. Lea: 2v., $1.75 each; $3.50 total.

SCHUBERT, Franz Peter, 1797-1828.
  164. [Quintet, violins, viola & violoncello, D. 956,
        C major] Quintet in C, Op. 163, D. 956. Boosey
        & Hawkes: $3.75. Eulenburg: $3.75. Kalmus:
        $1.50. Lea: with his piano quartet, D. 667,
        $1.75. Philharmonia: $2.25.

PIANO QUINTETS (2 violins, viola, violoncello, piano, unless otherwise specified)

BRAHMS, Johannes, 1833-1897.
165.   [Quintet, piano & strings, op. 34, F minor]
       Quintet in f for Piano & Strings, Op. 34.
       Eulenburg: $4.50. Kalmus: $2.00.

DVOŘÁK, Antonín, 1841-1904.
166.   [Quintet, piano & strings, op. 81, A major]
       Quintet in A, Op. 81 (piano). Eulenburg:
       $4.50.

SCHUBERT, Franz Peter, 1797-1828.
167.   [Quintet, piano, violin, viola, violoncello &
       double bass, D. 667, A major] Quintet in A
       (piano), Op. 114, "Trout," D. 667. Boosey &
       Hawkes: $3.75. Eulenburg: $3.00. Kalmus:
       $2.00. Lea: with his string quintet, D. 956,
       $1.75.

SCHUMANN, Robert Alexander, 1810-1856.
168.   [Quintet, piano & strings, op. 44, E flat major]
       Quintet in E flat for Piano & Strings, Op. 44.
       Eulenburg: $3.25. Kalmus: with his piano
       quartet, op. 47, $2.00.

STRING SEXTETS, OCTET

BRAHMS, Johannes, 1833-1897.
169.   [Sextets, violins, violas & violoncellos]
       Sextet in B flat for Strings, Op. 18; Sextet
       in G, Op. 36. Eulenburg: issued separately,
       $4.50 each; $9.00 total. Kalmus: $2.00.

MENDELSSOHN-BARTHOLDY, Felix, 1809-1847.
170.   [Octet, 4 violins, 2 violas & 2 violoncellos,
       op. 20, E flat major] Octet in E flat for
       Strings, Op. 20. Eulenburg: $3.25. Inter-
       national: $2.50. Kalmus: $2.00. Lea: with
       his string quintets, Op. 18, 87, $1.75.

SCHÖNBERG, Arnold, 1874-1951.
171.   [Verklärte Nacht] Verklärte Nacht, Op. 4 (1899)
       (sextet for violins, violas, violoncellos).
       International: $2.50. Kalmus: $2.00. Universal:
       $7.50.

COLLECTIONS (may be acquired in place of individual editions)

BEETHOVEN, Ludwig van, 1770-1827.
172. [Works, chamber music. Selections] Chamber music of Beethoven. Includes 4 string trios, 7 piano trios, 17 string quartets, piano quartet, string quintet, quintet for piano and winds, wind septet, wind octet, serenade for flute and strings. Belwin Mills: $5.95.

BRAHMS, Johannes, 1833-1897.
173. [Works, chamber music] Chamber music of Brahms. Complete for three or more instruments. Belwin Mills: $5.95. Eulenburg: 2v., bound, $20.00 each; $40.00 total.

174. [Works, chamber music. Selections] Chamber music for strings. Includes 3 string quartets, 2 string quintets, clarinet quintet, 2 string sextets. Kalmus: $4.00.

HAYDN, Joseph, 1732-1809.
175. [Works, chamber music. Selections] Chamber music of Haydn. Includes 26 string quartets and a piano trio. Belwin Mills: $5.95.

MENDELSSOHN-BARTHOLDY, Felix, 1809-1847.
176. [Works, chamber music. Selections] Octet and 2 string quintets. Lea: $1.75.

Miscellaneous Chamber Works.
177. Includes: BORODIN, A. P. Quartet, strings, no. 2, D major. DEBUSSY, C. Quartet strings, op. 10, G minor. DVOŘÁK, A. Quartets, strings, B. 92, E flat major; B. 179, F major; B. 192, G major. Quintet, violins, viola, violoncello & double bass, op. 81, A major. FAURÉ, G. U. Quartet, piano & strings, op. 15, C minor. FRANCK, C. A. Quintet, piano & strings, F minor. Quartet, strings, D major. GRIEG, E. H. Quartet, strings, op. 27, G minor. MENDELSSOHN-BARTHOLDY, F. Trio, piano & strings, op. 49, D minor. Quartets, strings, op. 12, E flat major; op. 44, no. 1, D major. SCHUMANN, R. A. Quartets, piano & strings, op. 44, E flat major;

op. 47, E flat major. Trio, piano & strings,
op. 63, D minor. Quartets, strings, op. 41,
no. 1, A minor; op. 41, no. 3, A major. SMETANA,
B. Quartet, strings, no. 1, E minor.
CHAĬKOVSKIĬ, P. I. Trio, piano & strings, op.
50, A minor. VERDI, G. Quartet, strings, E
minor. Belwin Mills: $5.95.

MOZART, Johann Chrysostom Wolfgang Amadeus, 1756-1791.
    178. [Works, chamber music. Selections] Chamber
Music of Mozart. Includes a string trio, 7
piano trios, 10 string quartets, 2 piano quartets, 2 flute quartets, oboe quartet, 6 string
quintets (Eine kleine Nachtmusik), clarinet
quintet, horn quintet, piano quintet, and horn
sextet (A Musical Joke). Belwin Mills: $5.95.

SCHUBERT, Franz Peter, 1797-1828.
    179. [Works, chamber music. Selections] Chamber
music of Schubert. Includes 2 piano trios, 5
string quartets, string quintet, piano quintet,
and octet. Belwin Mills: $5.95.

    180. [Works, chamber music. Selections] Chamber
music of Schubert. Includes 2 piano trios,
Nocturne, and Adagio & Rondo concertante.
Kalmus: 2v., $1.50 each; $3.00 total.

S T U D Y   S C O R E S:
C H A M B E R   M U S I C   W I T H   W I N D S

This list includes chamber music with wind instruments, with or without piano accompaniment. Arrangements and works including voice or narrator have been
excluded. Unless otherwise indicated, prices repre-
sent the approximate cost in 1978 of purchasing
paperbound editions. At the time of compilation, the
approximate cost of this entire list was $246.00, not
including items listed under "Collections." The
collective editions total $9.95-$44.00.

TRIOS

BARTÓK, Béla, 1881-1945.
   181.   [Contrasts] <u>Contrasts</u> for Clarinet, Violin,
          Piano (1938). Boosey & Hawkes: $6.00.

BEETHOVEN, Ludwig van, 1770-1827.
   182.   [Serenade, flute, violin & viola, op. 25, D
          major] Serenade in D for Flute, Violin, Viola,
          Op. 25. Eulenburg: $3.25. Lea: with his
          Sextet, Op. 71, $1.75.

   183.   [Trio, oboes & English horn, op. 87, C major]
          Trio in C for 2 Oboes and English Horn, Op. 87.
          Boosey & Hawkes: $1.25.

   184.   [Trio, piano, clarinet & violoncello, op. 11,
          B flat major] Trio in B flat, Op. 11. Kalmus:
          $2.00. See also STUDY SCORES: Chamber Music
          for Strings.

BRAHMS, Johannes, 1833-1897.
   185.   [Trio, piano, clarinet & violoncello, op. 114,
          A minor] Trio in a for Clarinet, Cello, Piano,
          Op. 114. Eulenburg: $3.75. Kalmus: $2.00.

186.   [Trio, piano, horn & violin, op. 40, E flat
       major]   Trio in E flat for Horn, Violin, Piano,
       Op. 40. Eulenburg: $3.75. Kalmus: $2.00.

DEBUSSY, Claude, 1862-1918.
187.   [Sonata, flute, viola & harp] Sonata No. 2
       for Flute, Viola and Harp (1916). Durand:
       $3.25.

MOZART, Johann Chrysostom Wolfgang Amadeus, 1756-1791.
188.   [Trio, piano, clarinet & viola, K. 498, E flat
       major] Trio in E flat for Clarinet, Viola,
       Piano, K. 498. Eulenburg: $3.25. Kalmus:
       $2.00. Lea: $1.75. See also STUDY SCORES:
       Chamber Music for Strings.

PISTON, Walter, 1894-   .
189.   [Pieces, flute, clarinet & bassoon]   3 Pieces
       for Flute, Clarinet & Bassoon (1925).
       Associated Music Publishers: $1.00.

POULENC, Francis, 1899-1963.
190.   [Sonata, trumpet, horn & trombone]   Sonata
       for Trumpet, Horn and Trombone. Chester:
       $2.50.

REGER, Max, 1873-1916.
191.   [Serenade, flute, violin & viola, op. 77a, D
       major] Serenade in D, flute, violin, viola,
       Op. 77a. Eulenburg: $4.50.

192.   [Serenade, flute, violin & viola, op. 141a,
       G major] Serenade in G, Flute, Violin, Viola,
       Op. 141a. Eulenburg: $3.75.

Quartets

CARTER, Elliott Cook, 1908-
193.   [Etudes and a fantasy, wood-winds] Eight
       Etudes & a Fantasy (1950) (flute, oboe, clari-
       net, bassoon). Associated Music Publishers:
       $4.00.

194.   [Sonata, harpsichord, wood-winds & violoncello]
       Sonata for Flute, Oboe, Cello, Harpsichord
       (1952). Associated Music Publishers: $3.50.

DEVIENNE, François, 1759-1803.
  195.   [Quartet, bassoon & strings, op. 73, no. 1, C
       major] Quartetti concertanti for Flute or
       Bassoon & Strings, Op. 73 (No. 1) (bassoon,
       violin, viola, violoncello). Musica Rara:
       $5.40.

HINDEMITH, Paul, 1895-1963.
  196.   [Plöner Musiktag. Morgenmusik] Morgenmusik
       (1932). (2 trumpets, 2 trombones, or other
       brass instruments). Schott: $3.00.

MOZART, Johann Chrysostom Wolfgang Amadeus, 1756-1791.
  197.   [Quartet, flute & strings, K. 285, D major]
       Quartet, Flute & Strings, K. 285 (flute,
       violin, viola, violoncello). Eulenburg:
       $3.25. Kalmus: $2.00.

  198.   [Quartet, flute & strings, K. 285a, G major]
       Quartet, Flute & Strings, K. 285a (flute,
       violin, viola, violoncello). Eulenburg:
       $2.00. Kalmus: $2.00.

  199.   [Quartet, flute & strings, K. 298, A major]
       Quartet, Flute & Strings, K. 298 (flute,
       violin, viola, violoncello). Eulenburg:
       $3.25. Kalmus: $2.00.

  200.   [Quartet, oboe & strings, K. 368b (370) F
       major] Quartet in F for Oboe & Strings, K.
       370 (oboe, violin, viola, violoncello).
       Boosey & Hawkes: $1.25. Eulenburg: $3.25.

QUINTETS (flute, oboe, clarinet, bassoon, horn, unless otherwise specified)

BEETHOVEN, Ludwig van, 1770-1827.
  201.   [Quintet, piano, wood-winds & horn, op. 16,
       E flat major] Quintet in E flat for Piano &
       Winds, Op. 16 (piano, oboe, clarinet, horn,
       bassoon). Eulenburg: $3.25. International:
       $2.00. Kalmus: $2.00. Lea: $1.75.

BRAHMS, Johannes, 1833-1897.
  202.   [Quintet, clarinet & strings, op. 115, B minor]
       Quintet in b for Clarinet and Strings, Op. 115

(clarinet, 2 violins, viola, violoncello).
Boosey & Hawkes: $3.50. Eulenburg: $3.75.

CARTER, Elliott Cook, 1809-
203. [Quintet, wood-winds & horn] Woodwind Quintet.
Associated Music Publishers: $1.50.

ETLER, Alvin Derald, 1913-1973.
204. [Quintet, wood-winds & horn, no. 1] Quintet
No. 1 for Winds. Associated Music Publishers:
$2.00.

205. [Sonic sequence] Sonic Sequence (1967) (2
trumpets, horn, 2 trombones). Alexander
Broude: $1.50.

FRANÇAIX, Jean, 1912-
206. [Quintet, wood-winds & horn] Quintet for
for Woodwinds (1948). Schott: $7.50.

GERHARD, Roberto, 1896-1970.
207. [Quintet, wood-winds & horn] Wind Quintet
(1928). Belwin-Mills: $3.50.

HENZE, Hans Werner, 1926-
208. [Quintet, wood-winds & horn] Wind Quintet
(1952). Schott: $6.00.

HINDEMITH, Paul, 1895-1963.
209. [Kleine Kammermusik, wood-winds & horn, Op.
24, no. 2] Kleine Kammermusik, Op. 24, No. 2
(1922). Schott: $6.00.

IBERT, Jacques, 1890-1962.
210. [Pièces brèves, wood-winds & horn] Trois
pièces brèves (1930). Leduc: $8.00.

MOZART, Johann Chrysostom Wolfgang Amadeus, 1756-1791.
211. [Quintet, clarinet & strings, K. 581, A major]
Quintet in A for Clarinet & Strings, K. 581
(clarinet, 2 violins, viola, violoncello).
Boosey & Hawkes: $3.00. Eulenburg: $3.25.
Kalmus: $2.00. Lea: $1.75.

212. [Quintet, horn & strings, K. 386c (407) E flat
major] Quintet in E flat for Horn and Strings,
K. 407 (horn, violin, 2 violas, violoncello).

Eulenburg: $3.25. Lea: $1.75. See also
STUDY SCORES: Chamber Music for Strings.

213. [Quintet, piano, wood-winds & horn, K. 452,
      E flat major] Quintet in E flat for Piano &
      Winds, K. 452 (oboe, clarinet, horn, bassoon,
      piano). Eulenburg: $3.25. International:
      $2.00. Kalmus: $2.00. Lea: $1.75.

NIELSEN, Carl, 1865-1931.
214. [Quintet, wood-winds & horn, op. 43] Quintet,
      Op. 43 (1922). W. Hansen: $5.00.

PROKOF'EV, Sergeĭ Sergeevich, 1891-1953.
215. [Quintet, oboe, clarinet & strings, op. 39]
      Quintet for Winds & Strings, Op. 39 (1924)
      (oboe, clarinet, violin, viola, double-bass).
      Boosey & Hawkes: $6.25. International: $3.00.

SCHÖNBERG, Arnold, 1874-1951.
216. [Quintet, wood-winds & horn, op. 26] Quintet
      for Flute, Oboe, Clarinet, Horn & Bassoon,
      Op. 26 (1924). Philharmonia: $7.50.

SCHULLER, Gunther,
217. [Quintet, wood-winds & horn] Woodwind Quintet
      (1958). Associated Music Publishers: $3.50.
      Schott: $3.00.

STOCKHAUSEN, Karlheinz, 1928-
218. [Zeitmasse] Nr. 2 Zeitmasse for Five Wood-
      winds (1957) (oboe, flute, English horn,
      clarinet, bassoon). Universal: $11.25.

SEXTETS

BEETHOVEN, Ludwig van, 1770-1827.
219. [Sextet, clarinets, bassoons & horns, op. 71,
      E flat major] Sextet in E flat for Winds,
      Op. 71. Eulenburg: $3.25. International:
      $2.00. Lea: with his Serenade, Op. 25, $1.75.

220. [Sextet, 2 horns & strings, op. 81b, E flat
      major] Sextet in E flat for 2 Horns & Strings,
      Op. 81b (2 horns, 2 violins, viola, violon-
      cello). Eulenburg: $3.25. Lea: with his
      Septet, Op. 20, $1.75.

FALLA, Manuel de, 1876-1946.
  221. [Concerto, harpsichord] Concerto in D for
        Harpsichord, Flute, Oboe, Clarinet, Violin &
        Violoncello. Eschig: $5.50.

JANÁČEK, Leoš, 1854-1928.
  222. [Mládí] Sextet for Wind instruments, "Youth"
        (1924) (flute, oboe, clarinet, horn, bassoon,
        bass clarinet). International: $3.00.

MOZART, Johann Chrysostom Wolfgang Amadeus, 1756-1791.
  223. [Divertimento, K. 213, F major] Divertimento
        No. 8 in F, K. 213 (2 oboes, 2 horns, 2
        bassoons). Eulenburg: $3.25. Kalmus: $2.00.

  224. [Divertimento, K. 240, B flat major] Diverti-
        mento No. 9 in B flat, K. 240 (2 oboes,
        2 horns, 2 bassoons). Eulenburg: $3.25.
        Kalmus: $2.00.

  225. [Divertimento, K. 240a (252) E flat major]
        Divertimento No. 12 in E flat, K. 252 (2 oboes,
        2 horns, 2 bassoons). Eulenburg: $3.25.
        Kalmus: $2.00.

  226. [Divertimento, K. 253, F major] Divertimento
        No. 13 in F, K. 253 (2 oboes, 2 horns, 2
        bassoons). Eulenburg: $3.25. Kalmus: $2.00.

  227. [Divertimento, K. 270, B flat major] Diverti-
        mento No. 14 in B flat, K. 270 (2 oboes, 2 horns,
        2 bassoons). Eulenburg: $3.25. Kalmus: $2.00.

  228. [Divertimento, K. 271b (287) B flat major]
        Divertimento No. 15 in B flat, K. 287 (2 horns,
        2 violins, viola, double bass). Eulenburg:
        $4.50.

  229. [Ein musikalischer Spass] Musical Joke, K. 522
        (2 horns, 2 violins, viola, violoncello).
        Eulenburg: $3.25.

POULENC, Francis, 1899-1963.
  230. [Sextet, piano, wood-winds & horn] Sextuor
        for Piano & Woodwind Quintet (1930-2) (flute,
        oboe, clarinet, bassoon, horn, piano). W.
        Hansen: $7.95.

ROCHBERG, George.
231. [Serenata d'estate] Serenata d'estate (flute,
      violin, viola, violoncello, guitar, harp).
      Leeds: $2.50.

XENAKIS, Iannis, 1922-
232. [Eonta] Eonta for piano and brass (1963) (2
      trumpets, 3 trombones, piano). Boosey &
      Hawkes: $12.00.

SEPTETS

BEETHOVEN, Ludwig van, 1770-1827.
233. [Septet, woodwinds, horn & strings, op. 20,
      E flat major] Septet in E flat for Strings
      & Winds, Op. 20 (clarinet, bassoon, horn,
      violin, viola, violoncello, double bass).
      Boosey & Hawkes: $1.50. Lea: with his Sextet,
      Op. 81b, $1.75. Philharmonia: $2.25.

RAVEL, Maurice, 1875-1937.
234. [Introduction et allegro, harp, wood-winds
      & strings] Introduction and Allegro for Harp,
      Flute, Clarinet & String Quartet (1905-06).
      Eulenburg: $6.75. International: $3.00.

SCHÖNBERG, Arnold, 1847-1951.
235. [Suite, piano, 3 clarinets & strings, op. 29]
      Suite for 2 Clarinets, Bass Clarinet, Violin,
      Viola, Cello & Piano, Op. 29 (1927). Phil-
      harmonia: $15.00.

STRAVINSKIĬ, Igor' Fedorovich, 1882-1971.
236. [Septet, piano, winds & strings] Septet for
      piano, string & wind instruments (1952)
      (clarinet, horn, bassoon, violin, viola,
      violoncello, piano). Boosey & Hawkes: $5.50.

OCTETS

BEETHOVEN, Ludwig van, 1770-1827.
237. [Octet, wood-winds & 2 horns, op. 103, E flat
      major] Octet in E flat for Winds, Op. 103
      (2 oboes, 2 clarinets, 2 bassoons, 2 horns).
      Eulenburg: $3.75.

238.   [Rondino, wood-winds & 2 horns, K. 25, E flat
        major] Rondino in E flat for Wind Octet,
        Gr. 146 (2 oboes, 2 clarinets, 2 bassoons,
        2 horns). Eulenburg: $2.75. International:
        $1.50. Kalmus: $2.00.

HINDEMITH, Paul, 1895-1963.
239.   [Octet, wood-winds, horn & strings] Octet
        (clarinet, horn, bassoon, violin, 2 violas,
        violoncello, double bass). Schott: $18.00.

MOZART, Johann Chrysostom Wolfgang Amadeus, 1756-1791.
240.   [Serenade, wood-winds & 2 horns, K. 375, E
        flat major] Serenade No. 11 in E flat, K.
        375 (2 oboes, 2 clarinets, 2 horns, 2 bassoons).
        Eulenburg: $3.75. Kalmus: $2.00.

SCHUBERT, Franz Peter, 1797-1828.
241.   [Octet, winds & strings, D. 803, F major]
        Octet in F for Strings & Winds, Op. 166,
        D. 803 (clarinet, horn, bassoon, 2 violins,
        viola, violoncello, double-bass). Boosey &
        Hawkes: $2.50. Eulenburg: $4.50. Kalmus:
        $2.00. Lea: $1.75.

STRAVINSKIĬ, Igor' Fedorovich, 1882-1971.
242.   [Octet, winds] Octet for Wind Instruments
        (1923) (flute, clarinet, 2 bassoons, 2 trum-
        pets, 2 trombones). Boosey & Hawkes: $6.00.

VARÈSE, Edgar, 1883-1965.
243.   [Octandre] Octandre. For eight instruments
        (1924) (flute, clarinet, oboe, bassoon, horn,
        trumpet, trombone, double-bass). G. Schirmer:
        $4.75.

COLLECTIONS (may be acquired in place of individual editions)

BEETHOVEN, Ludwig van, 1770-1827.
244.   [Works, chamber music. Selections] Chamber
        music for winds: includes Octet in E flat for
        Winds, Op. 103; Rondino in E flat for Wind
        Octet, Gr. 146; Sextet in E flat for Winds,
        Op. 71; Serenade in D for Flute, Violin, Viola,
        Op. 25; Trio in C for 2 Oboes and English Horn,

Op. 87; Duos (3) for Clarinet & Bassoon, G. 147.
Kalmus: $4.00.

BRAHMS, Johannes, 1833-1897.
  245. [Works, chamber music] Chamber music, complete:
        includes Quartets (3) (complete); Quintets
        No. 1 in F, Op. 88; No. 2 in G, Op. 111; Quin-
        tet in b for Clarinet and Strings, Op. 115;
        Sextet in B flat for Strings, Op. 18; Sextet
        in G, Op. 36; Trios (3) (piano) (complete);
        Quintet in f for Piano & Strings, Op. 34.
        Belwin-Mills: $5.95. Eulenburg: bound, 2v.,
        $20.00 each; $40.00 total. See also STUDY
        SCORES: Chamber Music for Strings.

PERFORMING EDITIONS: CHAMBER MUSIC FOR STRINGS

This list includes performing parts for string chamber music since 1750, for three to eight stringed instruments, with or without piano accompaniment. The pieces included are largely those which are commonly considered as belonging to the standard repertory for chamber music ensembles. Significant contemporary works have been included, provided the difficulty of performance does not exceed the capabilities of skilled amateur musicians. Adaptations, arrangements, juvenile and instructive editions have been excluded. Most of the works below also appear in the list STUDY SCORES: Chamber Music for Strings, and all works are available on commercial recordings. At the time of compilation the approximate cost of the entire list was $563.75, exclusive of the collective editions under "Collections" which cost $118.00.

STRING TRIOS (violin, viola, violoncello)

BEETHOVEN, Ludwig van, 1770-1827.
   246.   [Trios, strings] Trios (string) (5), Op. 3, 8 ("Serenade"), 9 (complete); Serenade in D for Flute, Violin, Viola, Op. 25. C. F. Peters: $9.00.

FINE, Irving Gifford.
   247.   [Fantasia, string trio] Fantasia for string trio. Belwin-Mills: $4.50, score included.

MOZART, Johann Chrysostom Wolfgang Amadeus, 1756-1791.
   248.   [Divertimento, string trio, K. 563, E flat major] Divertimento in E flat for String Trio, K. 563. Breitkopf & Hartel: $5.50. C. F. Peters: $4.00.

PIANO TRIOS (violin, violoncello, piano)

BEETHOVEN, Ludwig van, 1770-1827.
249. [Trios, piano & strings] Trios (piano) (13)
      (complete); Trio in B flat, Op. 11; Trio in G,
      Op. 121a (Kakadu); Variations in E flat, Op.
      44. G. Henle: 3v., $15.50, $16.00, $15.50;
      $47.00 total. C. F. Peters: 2v., $9.50, $8.00;
      $17.50 total.

BRAHMS, Johannes, 1833-1897.
250. [Trios, piano & strings] Trios (3) (piano)
      (complete). C. F. Peters: issued separately,
      $5.50 each; $16.50 total. G. Henle: $21.00.
      International: 3v., $4.50 each; $13.50 total.

DVOŘÁK, Antonín, 1841-1904.
251. [Trio, piano & strings, no. 4, op. 90, E minor]
      Trio in e, Op. 90, "Dumky." International:
      $7.50.

HAYDN, Joseph, 1732-1809.
252. [Trios, piano & strings] Trios (piano) (31).
      C. F. Peters: 3v., $11.00-$15.00 each; $41.00
      total.

IVES, Charles Edward, 1874-1954.
253. [Trio, piano & strings] Trio, for Violin, Cello,
      and Piano (1911). Peer International: $5.00.

MENDELSSOHN-BARTHOLDY, Felix, 1809-1847.
254. [Trios, piano & strings] Trio No. 1 in d
      (piano), Op. 49; Trio No. 2 in c (piano),
      Op. 66. G. Henle: $15.75. C. F. Peters:
      $10.00

MOZART, Johann Chrysostom Wolfgang Amadeus, 1756-1791.
255. [Trios, piano & strings] Trios (piano) (7),
      K. 254, 442, 496, 502, 542, 548, 564; includes
      also Trio in E flat for Clarinet, Viola, Piano,
      K. 498. G. Henle: $20.00. International:
      $10.00. C. F. Peters: (omits K. 442), $9.50.

RAVEL, Maurice, 1875-1937.
256. [Trio, piano & strings, A minor] Trio in a
      (piano) (1914). Durand: $17.75.

SCHUBERT, Franz Peter, 1797-1828.
257. [Adagio, piano trio, D. 897, E flat major]
       Nocturne in E flat, Op. 148, D. 897. Inter-
       national: $2.50.

258. [Trios, piano & strings] Trio No. 1 in B flat
       (piano), Op. 99, D. 898; Trio No. 2 in E flat
       (piano), Op. 100, D. 929. G. Henle: $17.50.
       C. F. Peters: $8.50.

SCHUMANN, Robert Alexander, 1810-1856.
259. [Trios, piano & strings] Trios (3) for Violin,
       Cello, Piano, Op. 63, 80, 110. C. F. Peters:
       $15.00.

SHOSTAKOVICH, Dmitriĭ Dmitrievich, 1906-   .
260. [Trio, piano & strings, no. 2, op. 67, E minor]
       Trio No. 2 in e (piano), Op. 67 (1944).
       International: $6.00. C. F. Peters: $15.00.

SMETANA, Bedřich, 1824-1884.
261. [Trio, piano & strings, op. 15, G minor] Trio
       in g (piano), Op. 15. International: $6.00.
       C. F. Peters: $9.50.

STRING QUARTETS (2 violins, viola, violoncello)

BARTÓK, Béla, 1881-1945.
262. [Quartet, strings, no. 1] Quartet No. 1 (Op.
       7). Boosey & Hawkes: $10.00. International:
       $6.00.

BEETHOVEN, Ludwig van, 1770-1827.
263. [Quartets, strings] Quartets (17) (complete).
       G. Henle: 2v.; $16.75, $17.25; $34.00 total.
       C. F. Peters: 3v., $9.00-$11.00 each; $29.00
       total.

BORODIN, Aleksandr Porfir'evich, 1833-1887.
264. [Quartet, strings, no. 2, D major] Quartet
       No. 2 in D. Breitkopf & Härtel: $6.00.
       International: $6.00. Kalmus: $3.75.

BRAHMS, Johannes, 1833-1897.
265. [Quartet, strings] Quartets (3) (complete).
       Breitkopf & Härtel: issued separately, $4.75

each; $14.25 total. International: $7.50.
C. F. Peters: $8.00.

DEBUSSY, Claude, 1862-1918.
   266. [Quartet, strings, op. 10, G minor] Quartet
         in g, Op. 10 (1893). Durand: $11.50. Inter-
         national: $5.00.

DVOŘÁK, Antonín, 1841-1904.
   267. [Quartet, strings, B. 75, D minor] Quartet No.
         2 in d, Op. 34. Artia: $5.50.

   268. [Quartet, strings, B. 92, E flat major] Quar-
         tet No. 3 in E flat, Op. 51. Artia: $6.00.
         International: $6.00.

   269. [Quartet, strings, B. 121, C major] Quartet
         No. 4 in C, Op. 61. Artia: $6.00. Brietkopf
         & Härtel: $6.75. International: $6.00.

   270. [Quartet, strings, B. 179, F major] Quartet
         No. 6 in F, Op. 96, "American," Artia: $6.00.
         Breitkopf & Härtel: $9.50. International:
         $6.00.

   271. [Quartet, strings, B. 192, G major] Quartet
         No. 8 in G, Op. 106. Artia: $6.00. Inter-
         national: $6.00.

   272. [Quartet, strings, B. 193, A flat major] Quar-
         tet No. 7 in A flat, Op. 105. Artia: $6.00.
         International: $6.00.

HAYDN, Joseph, 1732-1809.
   273. [Quartets, strings. Selections] Quartets
         Op. 3, No. 3; Op. 3, No. 5; Op. 9, No. 2;
         Op. 17, No. 5; Op. 20, Nos. 4-6; Op. 33, Nos.
         2-3; Op. 33, No. 6; Op. 50, No. 6; Op. 54,
         No. 13; Op. 64, Nos. 2-6; Op. 74, Nos. 1-3;
         Op. 76, Nos. 1-6; Op. 77, Nos. 1-2. G. Henle:
         3v., (early works, Op. 9, Op. 17) $22.00,
         $16.00, $22.00; $60.00 total. International:
         2v., $13.75 each; $27.50 total. C. F. Peters:
         2v., $11.00 each; $22.00 total.

IVES, Charles Edward, 1874-1954.
  274. [Quartet strings, no. 1] Quartet No. 1 (1896).
        Peer International: $6.00.

  275. [Quartet, strings, no. 2] Quartet No. 2 (1913).
        Peer International: $10.00.

MENDELSSOHN-BARTHOLDY, Felix, 1809-1847.
  276. [Quartets, strings] Quartets (7), Op. 12, 13,
        44, 44a, 44b, 80, 81. C. F. Peters: $11.00.

MOZART, Johann Chrysostom Wolfgang Amadeus, 1756-1791.
  277. [Quartets, strings] Quartets; Serenade in G,
        K. 525, "Eine kleine Nachtmusik;" includes
        also Quartet, Flute & Strings, K. 298; Quar-
        tet in F for Oboe & Strings, K. 370; Adagio
        and Fugue in c, K. 546. C. F. Peters: 2v.,
        $11.00 each; $22.00 total.

NIELSEN, Carl, 1865-1931.
  278. [Quartet, strings, no. 4, op. 44, F major]
        Quartet Op. 44. C. F. Peters: $8.50.

PROKOF'EV, Sergeĭ Sergeevich, 1891-1953.
  279. [Quartet, strings, no. 1, op. 50] Quartet
        No. 1, Op. 50 (1931). Boosey & Hawkes: $11.75.
        International: $6.00.

  280. [Quartet, strings, no. 2, op. 92] Quartet No.
        2, Op. 92 (1941). International: $5.00.
        C. F. Peters: $13.50.

RAVEL, Maurice, 1875-1937.
  281. [Quartet, strings, F major] Quartet in F
        (1902-1903). Durand: $15.75. International:
        $5.00.

SCHUBERT, Franz Peter, 1797-1828.
  282. [Quartets, strings. Selections] Quartets No.
        10 in E flat, Op. 125, No. 1, D. 87; No. 7 in
        D, D. 94; No. 8 in B flat, Op. 168, D. 112;
        No. 9 in g, D. 173; No. 11 in E, Op. 125, No.
        2, D. 353; No. 12 in c, "Quartettsatz," D. 703;
        No. 13 in a, Op. 29, D. 804; No. 14 in d,
        "Death and the Maiden," D. 810, No. 15 in G,
        Op. 161, D. 887. C. F. Peters: 2v., $8.50,
        $9.00; $17.50 total.

SCHUMANN, Robert Alexander, 1810-1856.
  283. [Quartets, strings] Quartets (3), Op. 41 (com-
        plete). Breitkopf & Härtel: issued separately,
        $3.50-$5.50 each; $12.50 total. International:
        $7.50. C. F. Peters: $8.50.

SMETANA, Bedřich, 1824-1884.
  284. [Quartet, strings, no. 1, E minor] Quartet
        No. 1 in e, "From my Life." International:
        $6.00. C. F. Peters: $5.00.

STRAVINSKIĬ, Igor' Fedorovich, 1882-1971.
  285. [Double canon, string quartet] Double Canon
        for String Quartet (1959). 4 scores required
        for performance. Boosey & Hawkes: $3.00
        each; $12.00 total.

  286. [Pieces, string quartet] 3 Pieces for String
        Quartet (1914). Boosey & Hawkes: $8.00.
        International: $3.75.

WEBERN, Anton von, 1883-1945.
  287. [Bagatelles, string quartet, op. 9] Six
        Bagatelles for String Quartet, Op. 9 (1913).
        Universal: $3.50.

  288. [Langsamer Satz, string quartet] Slow Move-
        ment, for Quartet (1905). Boosey & Hawkes:
        $4.25. Carl Fischer: $3.00.

  289. [Quartet, strings (1905)] Quartet (1905).
        Boosey & Hawkes: $7.00. Carl Fischer: $4.50.

  290. [Sätze, string quartet, op. 5] <u>Five Movements</u>
        <u>for String Quartet</u>, Op. 5 (1909). Universal:
        $4.50.

PIANO QUARTETS (violin, viola, violoncello, piano)

BRAHMS, Johannes, 1833-1897.
  291. [Quartets, piano & strings] Quartets (3) for
        Piano and Strings (complete). International:
        issued separately, $7.50 each; $22.50 total.
        G. Henle: 3v., $12.00, $10.75, $12.00; $34.75
        total. C. F. Peters: 3v., $7.50 each; $22.50
        total.

MOZART, Johann Chrysostom Wolfgang Amadeus, 1756-1791.
292. [Quartets, piano & strings] Quartets (piano)
in g, K. 478; in E flat, K. 493. G. Henle:
$10.50. C. F. Peters: $6.50.

SCHUMANN, Robert Alexander, 1810-1856.
293. [Quartet, piano & strings, op. 47, E flat major]
Quartet in E flat for Piano & Strings, Op. 47.
International: $5.00. C. F. Peters: $7.00.

STRING QUINTETS

BEETHOVEN, Ludwig van, 1770-1827.
294. [Quintet, violins, violas & violoncello, op. 29,
C major] Quintet in C, Op. 29. Breitkopf &
Härtel: $6.00. International: $3.50. G. Henle:
$16.50 (complete quintets). C. F. Peters:
$8.50 (complete quintets).

BRAHMS, Johannes, 1833-1897.
295. [Quintet, violins, violas & violoncello, no. 1,
op. 88, F major] Quintet No. 1 in F, Op. 88.
International: $5.00. C. F. Peters: $6.00.

296. [Quintet, violins, violas & violoncello, no. 2,
op. 111, G major] Quintet No. 2 in G, Op. 111.
International: $5.00. C. F. Peters: $6.00.

DVOŘÁK, Antonín, 1841-1904.
297. [Quintet, violins, violas & violoncello, op. 97,
E flat major] Quintet No. 3 in E flat, Op. 97
(strings). Artia: $8.00. Breitkopf & Härtel:
$6.00. International: $7.50.

298. [Quintet, violins, viola, violoncello & double
bass, op. 77, G major] Quintet in G, Op. 77
(orig. Op. 18). Artia: $7.50. International:
$7.50.

MOZART, Johann Chrysostom Wolfgang Amadeus, 1756-1791.
299. [Quintets, violins, violas & violoncello]
Quintets (6) K. 174, 406, 515, 516, 593, 614;
Quintet No. 1 in F flat, K. 46; includes also
Quintet in A for Clarinet & Strings, K. 581;
Quintet in E flat for Horn and Strings, K. 407.
C. F. Peters: 2v., $9.00 each; $18.00 total.

SCHUBERT, Franz Peter, 1797–1828.
  300. [Quintet, violins, viola & violoncellos,
        D. 956, C major] Quintet in C, Op. 163,
        D. 956. International: $5.00. C. F. Peters:
        $6.00.

PIANO QUINTETS (2 violins, viola, violoncello, piano, unless otherwise specified)

BRAHMS, Johannes, 1833–1897.
  301. [Quintet, piano & strings, op. 34, F minor]
        Quintet in f for Piano & strings, Op. 34.
        Breitkopf & Härtel: $9.50. G. Henle: $14.50.
        International: $7.50. C. F. Peters: $7.50.

DVOŘÁK, Antonín, 1841–1904.
  302. [Quintet, piano & strings, op. 81, A major]
        Quintet in A, Op. 81 (piano). International:
        $8.50.

SCHUBERT, Franz Peter, 1797–1828.
  303. [Quintet, piano, violin, viola, violoncello
        & double bass, D. 667, A major] Quintet in
        A (piano), Op. 114, "Trout," D. 667. Breit-
        kopf & Härtel: $8.50. International: $7.50.
        C. F. Peters: $6.00.

SCHUMANN, Robert Alexander, 1810–1856.
  304. [Quintet, piano & strings, op. 44, E flat major]
        Quintet in E flat for Piano & Strings, Op. 44.
        Breitkopf & Härtel: $8.50. International:
        $7.50. C. F. Peters: $8.00.

STRING SEXTETS, OCTET

BRAHMS, Johannes, 1833–1897.
  305. [Sextets, violins, violas & violoncellos] Sex-
        tet in B flat for Strings, Op. 18; Sextet in G,
        Op. 36. International: issued separately,
        $7.50 each; $15.00 total. C. F. Peters: issued
        separately, $7.00, $7.50 each; $14.50 total.

MENDELSSOHN-BARTHOLDY, Felix, 1809–1847.
  306. [Octet, 4 violins, 2 violas & 2 violoncellos,
        op. 20, E flat major] Octet in E flat for
        Strings, Op. 20. International: $7.50. C. F.
        Peters: $8.50.

SCHÖNBERG, Arnold, 1874-1951.
307. [Verklärte Nacht] Verklärte Nacht, Op. 4
(1899) (sextet for violins, violas, violoncellos). International: $7.50.

COLLECTIONS (may be acquired in place of individual editions)

BEETHOVEN, Ludwig van, 1770-1827.
308. [Quartets, strings] Complete string quartets.
Reprint of the Breitkopf & Härtel edition.
Four scores required for performance. Dover:
$6.95 each; $27.80 total.

BRAHMS, Johannes, 1833-1897.
309. [Works, chamber music. Selections] Complete
chamber music for strings and clarinet quintet.
Reprint of the Vienna Gesellschaft der Musik-
freunde edition of the quartets, quintets,
and sextet without piano. Five scores required
for performance. Dover: $4.00 each; $20.00
total.

MOZART, Johann Chrysostom Wolfgang Amadeus, 1756-1791.
310. [Quartets, strings] Complete string quartets.
Reprint of the Breitkopf & Härtel edition.
Four scores required for performance. Dover.
$5.00 each; $25.00 total.

SCHUBERT, Franz Peter, 1797-1828.
311. [Works, chamber music. Selections] Complete
chamber music for pianoforte and strings.
Includes the "Trout" quintet, quartet in F major,
and three piano trios. Five scores required for
performance. Dover: $4.50 each; $22.50 total.

312. [Works, chamber music. Selections] Complete
chamber music for strings. Includes the
quintet in C major, the 15 quartets, and two
trios for string. Five scores required for
performance. Dover: $4.50 each; $22.50 total.

PERFORMING EDITIONS:
CHAMBER MUSIC WITH WINDS

This list includes performing parts for chamber
music with wind instruments since 1750, for three to
eight performers, with or without piano accompaniment.
The pieces included are largely those which are
commonly considered as belonging to the standard
repertory for wind chamber music ensembles. Significant contemporary works have been included, provided
the difficulty of performance does not exceed the
capability of skilled amateur chamber musicians. At
the time of compilation the approximate cost of the
entire list was $373.75.

TRIOS

BARTÓK, Béla, 1881-1945.
313. [Contrasts] <u>Contrasts</u> for Clarinet, Violin,
Piano (1938). Boosey & Hawkes: $23.50.

BEETHOVEN, Ludwig van, 1770-1827.
314. [Serenade, flute, violin & viola, op. 25, D
major] Serenade in D for Flute, Violin, Viola,
Op. 25. C. F. Peters: $9.00.

315. [Trio, oboes & English horn, op. 87, C major]
Trio in C for 2 Oboes and English horn, Op.
87. Boosey & Hawkes: $6.25, with miniature
score. C. F. Peters: $4.00.

316. [Trio, piano, clarinet & violoncello, op. 11,
B flat major] Trio in B flat, Op. 11. Breitkopf & Härtel: $4.50. C. F. Peters: $9.50.
<u>See also</u> PERFORMING EDITIONS: Chamber Music
for Strings.

BRAHMS, Johannes, 1833-1897.
  317. [Trio, piano, clarinet & violoncello, op. 114,
        A minor] Trio in a for Clarinet, Cello, Piano,
        Op. 114. Breitkopf & Härtel: $6.00. C. F.
        Peters: $5.50.

  318. [Trio, piano, violin & horn, op. 40, E flat
        major] Trio in E flat for Horn, Violin,
        Piano, Op. 40. C. F. Peters: $5.50.

IVES, Charles Edward, 1874-1954.
  319. [Largo, piano, clarinet, violin] Largo for
        Violin, Clarinet & Piano (1902). Southern
        (San Antonio, Texas): $2.75. Score and parts.

MOZART, Johann Chrysostom Wolfgang Amadeus, 1756-1791.
  320. [Trio, piano, clarinet & viola, K. 498, E flat
        major] Trio in E flat for Clarinet, Viola,
        Piano, K. 498. Breitkopf & Härtel: $4.75.
        International: $10.00 (8 trios). Philharmonia:
        $9.50 (7 trios). See also PERFORMING EDITIONS:
        Chamber Music for Strings.

PISTON, Walter, 1894-
  321. [Pieces, flute, clarinet & bassoon] 3 Pieces
        for Flute, Clarinet & Bassoon (1925). Asso-
        ciated Music Publishers: no price.

POULENC, Francis, 1899-1963.
  322. [Sonata, trumpet, horn & trombone] Sonata for
        Trumpet, Horn and Trombone. Chester: $5.00.

QUARTETS

CARTER, Elliott Cook, 1908-
  323. [Etudes and a fantasy, wood-winds] Eight
        Etudes & Fantasy (1950) (flute, oboe, clarinet,
        bassoon). Associated Music Publishers: no
        price.

DANZI, Franz, 1763-1826.
  324. [Quartet, bassoon & strings, op. 40, no. 1,
        C major] Quartets (2) for Bassoon & Strings,
        Op. 40 (No. 1). Musica Rara: $10.75.

DEVIENNE, François, 1759-1803.
325. [Quartet, bassoon & strings, op. 73, no. 1, C
major] Quartetti concertanti for flute or
bassoon & strings, Op. 73 (No. 1) (bassoon,
violin, viola, violoncello). Musica Rara:
$10.50. G. Schirmer: $4.00.

HINDEMITH, Paul, 1895-1963.
326. [Plöner Musiktag. Morgenmusik] Morgenmusik
(1932) (2 trumpets, 2 trombones; or other
brass instruments). Schott: $2.50.

MESSIAEN, Oliver, 1908-
327. [Quatuor pour la fin du temps] Quatuor pour
la fin du temps (clarinet, violin, violoncello,
piano). Durand: $28.25.

MOZART, Johann Chrysostom Wolfgang Amadeus, 1756-1791.
328. [Quartets, flute & strings] Quartets, Flute &
Strings, K. 285, 285a, 285b, 298 (flute, violin,
viola, violoncello). International: $6.00.
G. Schirmer: 2v., $3.50, $6.00; $9.00 total.
See also PERFORMING EDITIONS: Chamber Music
for Strings.

QUINTETS (flute, oboe, clarinet, bassoon, horn, unless otherwise specified)

BARBER, Samuel, 1910-
329. [Summer music] Summer Music for Woodwind Qn,
Op. 31 (1956). G. Schirmer: $3.50, score
included.

BEETHOVEN, Ludwig van, 1770-1827.
330. [Quintet, piano, wood-winds & horn, op. 16,
E flat major] Quintet in E flat for Piano &
Winds, Op. 16 (piano, oboe, clarinet, horn,
bassoon). G. Henle: $7.75. Kalmus: $5.00.
C. F. Peters: $5.00.

BRAHMS, Johannes, 1833-1897.
331. [Quintet, clarinet & strings, op. 115, B minor]
Quintet in b for Clarinet & Strings, Op. 115
(clarinet, 2 violins, viola, violoncello).
Boosey & Hawkes: $9.00, with miniature score.
Breitkopf & Härtel: $6.00. C. F. Peters: $6.50.

CARTER, Elliott Cook, 1908-
    332. [Quintet, wood-winds & horn] Woodwind Quartet
          (1948). Associated Music Publishers: no price.

CHAVEZ, Carlos, 1899-
    333. [Soli, no. 2, wood-winds & horn] Woodwind
          Quintet (1943). Associated Music Publishers:
          no price.

COWELL, Henry, 1897-1965.
    334. [Ballad, woodwinds & horn] Ballad. Associated
          Music Publishers: no price.

DANZI, Franz, 1763-1826.
    335. [Quintet, wood-winds & horn, op. 67, no. 2, E
          minor] Quintets for Woodwind, Op. 67 (No. 2).
          International: $7.50. G. Schirmer: $6.00.

ETLER, Alvin Derald, 1913-1973.
    336. [Quintet, brasses] Quintet for Brass Instruments
          (1964) (2 trumpets, horn, trombone, tuba).
          Associated Music Publishers: $6.00.

    337. [Sonic sequence] Sonic Sequence (1967) (2
          trumpets, horn, 2 trombones). Alexander
          Broude: $7.50.

FINE, Irving Gifford.
    338. [Partita, wood-winds & horn] Partita for Wind
          Quintet (1948). Boosey & Hawkes: $9.50.

FRANÇAIX, Jean, 1912-
    339. [Quintet, wood-winds & horn] Quintet for
          Woodwinds (1948). Schott: $16.50.

HENZE, Hans Werner, 1926-
    340. [Quintet, wood-winds & horn] Wind quintet
          (1952). Schott: $14.00.

HINDEMITH, Paul, 1895-1963.
    341. [Kleine Kammermusik, wood-winds & horn, op. 24,
          no. 2] Kleine Kammermusik, Op. 24, No. 2
          (1922). Schott: $7.50.

IBERT, Jacques, 1890-1962.
    342. [Pièces brèves, wood-winds & horn] Trois
          pièces brèves (1930). Leduc: $8.00.

MILHAUD, Darius, 1892-
343. [La cheminée du roi René] Cheminée du Roi
René, Op. 205 (1939). Southern (San Antonio,
Texas): $4.00.

MOZART, Johann Chrysostom Wolfgang Amadeus, 1756-1791.
344. [Quintet, clarinet & strings, K. 581, A major]
Quintet in A for Clarinet & Strings, K. 581
(clarinet, 2 violins, viola, violoncello).
Breitkopf & Härtel: $4.75. C. F. Peters:
$9.00.

345. [Quintet, horn & strings, K. 386c (407), E flat
major] Quintet in E flat for Horn and Strings,
K. 407 (horn, violin, 2 violas, violoncello).
C. F. Peters: with Quintet K. 581, no price.
See also PERFORMING EDITIONS: Chamber Music
for Strings.

346. [Quintet, piano, wood-winds & horn, K. 452,
E flat major] Quintet in E flat for Piano &
Winds, K. 452 (oboe, clarinet, horn, bassoon,
piano). Breitkopf & Härtel: $11.25. Inter-
national: $5.00.

NIELSEN, Carl, 1865-1931.
347. [Quintet, wood-winds & horn, op. 43] Quintet,
Op. 43 (1922). W. Hansen: $7.50.

PROKOF'EV, Sergeĭ Sergeevich, 1891-1953.
348. [Quintet, oboe, clarinet & strings, op. 39]
Quintet for Winds & Strings, Op. 39 (1924)
(oboe, clarinet, violin, viola, double bass).
Boosey & Hawkes: $19.00. International: $7.50.

REICHA, Anton Joseph, 1770-1936.
349. [Quintet, wood-winds & horn, op. 91, no. 1,
C major] Quintet in C, Op. 91, No. 1.
Kneusslin: $6.00.

350. [Quintet, wood-winds & horn, op. 100, no. 4,
E minor] Quintet in e, Op. 100, No. 4.
Kneusslin: $7.50.

SCHULLER, Gunther.
351. [Quintet, wood-winds & horn] Woodwind Quintet
(1958). Schott: $5.00.

WEBER, Karl Maria Friedrich Ernst, Freiherr von, 1786-
1826.
352. [Quintet, clarinet & strings, op. 34, B flat
major] Quintet (clarinet) in B flat, Op. 34
(clarinet, 2 violins, viola, violoncello).
Breitkopf & Härtel: $11.25. Musica Rara:
$2.25.

SEXTETS

BEETHOVEN, Ludwig van, 1770-1827.
353. [Sextet, clarinets, bassoons & horns, op. 71,
E flat major] Sextet in E flat for Winds, Op.
71. Breitkopf & Härtel: $4.50. International:
$7.00. C. F. Peters: $12.50.

354. [Sextet, 2 horns & strings, op. 81b, E flat
major] Sextet in E flat for 2 Horns & Strings,
Op. 81b (2 horns, 2 violins, viola, violoncello).
International: $3.75. C. F. Peters: $4.50.

JANÁČEK, Leoš, 1954-1928.
355. [Mládí] Sextet for Wind Instruments, "Youth"
(1924) (flute, oboe, clarinet, horn, bassoon,
bass clarinet). International: $7.50.

MOZART, Johann Chrysostom Wolfgang Amadeus, 1756-1791.
356. [Divertimento, K. 213, F major] Divertimento
No. 8 in F, K. 213 (2 oboes, 2 horns, 2
bassoons). Breitkopf & Härtel: $5.75. Kalmus:
$5.00.

357. [Divertimento, K. 240, B flat major] Divertimento No. 9 in B flat, K. 240 (2 oboes, 2 horns,
2'bassoons). Breitkopf & Härtel: $5.75.
Kalmus: $5.00.

358. [Divertimento, K. 240a (252) E flat major]
Divertimento No. 12 in E flat, K. 252 (2 oboes,
2 horns, 2 bassoons). Breitkopf & Härtel:
$5.75. Kalmus: $5.00.

359. [Divertimento, K. 253, F major] Divertimento
No. 3 in F, K. 253 (2 oboes, 2 horns, 2
bassoons). Breitkopf & Härtel: $5.75.
Kalmus: $5.00.

360. [Divertimento, K. 270, B flat major] Divertimento No. 14 in B flat, K. 270 (2 oboes,
2 horns, 2 bassoons). Breitkopf & Härtel:
$5.75. Kalmus: $5.00.

361. [Divertimento, K. 271g (289) E flat major]
Divertimento No. 16 in E flat, K. 289 (2 oboes,
2 horns, 2 bassoons). Breitkopf & Härtel:
$5.75. Kalmus: $5.00.

362. [Ein musikalischer Spass] Musical Joke, K. 522
(2 horns, 2 violins, viola, violoncello).
Kalmus: $5.00.

POULENC, Francis, 1899-1963.
363. [Sextet, piano, wood-winds & horn] Sextuor
for Piano & Woodwind Quintet (1930-2) (flute,
oboe, clarinet, bassoon, horn, piano).
W. Hansen: $19.75, score and parts.

SEPTET

BEETHOVEN, Ludwig van, 1770-1827.
364. [Septet, wood-winds, horn & strings, op. 20,
E flat major] Septet in E flat for Strings &
Winds, Op. 20 (clarinet, bassoon, horn, violin,
viola, violoncello, double-bass). C. F.
Peters: $7.00.

OCTETS

BEETHOVEN, Ludwig van, 1770-1827.
365. [Octet, wood-winds & 2 horns, op. 103, E flat
major] Octet in E flat for Winds, Op. 103
(2 oboes, 2 clarinets, 2 bassoons, 2 horns).
Breitkopf & Härtel: $7.50.

366. [Rondino, wood-winds & 2 horns, K. 25, E flat
major] Rondino in E flat for Wind Octet, Gr.
146 (2 oboes, 2 clarinets, 2 bassoons, 2 horns).
Breitkopf & Härtel: $4.00. International:
$4.50.

MOZART, Johann Chrysostom Wolfgang Amadeus, 1756-1791.
367. [Serenade, wood-winds & 2 horns, K. 375, E flat
major] Serenade No. 11 in E flat, K. 375

(2 oboes, 2 clarinets, 2 horns, 2 bassoons).
Breitkopf & Härtel: $13.50.

SCHUBERT, Franz Peter, 1797-1828.
  368. [Octet, winds & strings, D. 803, F major] Octet
        in F for Strings & Winds, Op. 166, D. 803
        (clarinet, horn, bassoon, 2 violins, viola,
        violoncello, double-bass). C. F. Peters: $8.50.

STRAVINSKIĬ, Igor' Fedorovich, 1882-1971.
  369. [Octet, winds] Octet for Wind Instruments
        (1923) (flute, clarinet, 2 bassoons, 2 trum-
        pets, 2 trombones). Breitkopf & Härtel: $12.50.
        Boosey & Hawkes: $10.00.

PERFORMING EDITIONS:
SONGS FOR SOLO VOICE WITH PIANO OR ORCHESTRA

This list includes primarily performing editions for individual songs and song cycles whether accompanied by piano or orchestra. In a few cases, study scores are cited as well since vocal music is otherwise omitted from the study score lists in this monograph. The pieces included are largely those which are considered part of the standard repertoire for solo voice. Significant works from the twentieth century have been included.

Many vocal works are published with translations of the original texts. In this list languages are indicated by the following abbreviations: C, Czech; E, English; F, French; G. German; I, Italian; P, Portugese; R, Russian; S, Spanish. Also, if the work is available in various transpositions, the ranges are indicated as low, medium, or high voice; the work is published separately in these ranges and should be ordered separately.

At the time of compilation (1978) the approximate cost of the list was $506.50 with the following distribution: individual songs and cycles, $300.00; anthologies, $56.60; aria collections, $80.00 if both sets are purchased; and folk song collections, $70.00. These cost quotations cover only one copy of each title rather than a copy for each voice range published. A small library might wish to consider collections of songs prior to the purchase of individual pieces.

INDIVIDUAL SONGS AND SONG CYCLES

BARBER, Samuel, 1910–
   370. [Songs. Selections] Collected Songs. G.
         Schirmer: high or low voice, (E), $5.00 each.

BEETHOVEN, Ludwig van, 1770-1827.
    Performing edition:
    371. [Songs. Selections] Thirty Selected Songs.
        Edited by Friedlander. C. F. Peters: high,
        medium, or low voice, (G), $5.75 each.

    Study score:
    372. [Songs. Selections] Lieder for Voice and
        Piano. Lea: (G, E), $1.50.

BERG, Alban, 1885-1935.
    373. [Orchester-Lieder, op. 4] Altenberg Lieder,
        Op. 4. Universal: (G), $4.25.

BERIO, Luciano, 1925-
    374. [Circles] Circles, for Female Voice, Harp,
        and 2 Percussion Players. Boosey & Hawkes
        (Suvini Zerboni): $8.00.

BERLIOZ, Hector, 1803-1869.
    375. [Les nuits d'été] Nuits d'été, Op. 7. Inter-
        national: high or low voice, (F, E), $3.00
        each.

BRAHMS, Johannes, 1833-1897.
    Performing edition:
    376. [Songs. Selections] 70 Songs. Edited by
        Sergius Kagen. International: high or low
        voice, (G, E), $7.50 each.

    Study score:
    377. [Songs. Selections] Lieder for Voice and
        Piano. Vol. 7. Includes Op. 105; Op. 106;
        Op. 107; Ernste Gesänge, Op. 121; Zigeuner-
        lieder; Nachgelassene Volkslieder. Lea:
        (G), $1.50.

BRITTEN, Benjamin, 1913-1976.
    378. [Serenade, tenor, horn & string orchestra,
        op. 31] Serenade for Tenor, Horn, Strings,
        Op. 31 (1943). Boosey & Hawkes: (E), $5.00.

CHAĬKOVSKIĬ, Petr Il'ich, 1840-1893.
    379. [Songs. Selections] 12 Songs. G. Schirmer:
        (G, E), $1.50, high voice; $1.25, low voice.

CHAUSSON, Ernest, 1855-1899.
  380. [Songs. Selections] 20 Songs. Edited by
       Sergius Kagen. International: high or low
       voice, (F, E), $4.00 each.

COPLAND, Aaron, 1900-
  381. [Poems of Emily Dickinson] Twelve Poems of
       Emily Dickinson for Voice and Piano (1948-50).
       Boosey & Hawkes: (E), $5.00.

CRUMB, George.
  382. [Ancient voices of children] Ancient Voices
       of Children, for Soprano, Boy Soprano, Oboe,
       Mandolin, Harp, Toy Piano, Electric Piano, and
       Percussion. C. F. Peters: (E), $12.50.

DALLAPICCOLA, Luigi, 1904-1975.
  383. [Goethe Lieder] Goethe-Lieder for Mezzo-
       soprano and 3 Clarinets. Boosey & Hawkes
       (Suvini Zerboni): $8.00.

DEBUSSY, Claude, 1862-1918.
  384. [Songs. Selections] 43 Songs. Edited by
       Sergius Kagen. International: (F, E), $7.50.

DOWLAND, John, 1563-1625.
  385. [Works. Selections; arr.] 50 Songs, Piano
       Accompaniment. Lute Songs. Edited by Edmund
       Fellowes. Revised by D. Scott. Stainer &
       Bell: high, medium, or low voice, (E), 2v.,
       $3.50 each; $7.00 total for each voice range.

DUPARC, Henri, 1848-1933.
  386. [Songs. Selections] 12 Songs, for Voice and
       Piano. Edited by Sergius Kagen. International:
       high, medium, or low voice, (F, E), $4.00
       each.

DVOŘÁK, Antonín, 1841-1904.
  387. [Biblische Lieder] Biblical Songs, Op. 99.
       International: high and low voice, (C, G, E),
       2v., $2.00 each; $4.00 total for each voice
       range.

FALLA, Manuel de, 1876-1946.
   388. [Canciones populares españolas] <u>Seven Popular</u>
      <u>Spanish Songs</u> (1914). Eschig: high or medium
      voice, (S, E, F), $2.50 each.

FAURÉ, Gabriel Urbain, 1945-1924.
   389. [Songs. Selections] 30 Songs. International:
      high, medium, or medium-high voice, (F, E),
      $5.00 each.

FOSTER, Stephen Collins, 1826-1864.
   390. [Songs. Selections] <u>Household Songs</u>. Earlier
      American Music, 12. Da Capo: (E), $12.50.

GRANADOS y Campiña, Enrique, 1867-1916.
   391. [Tonadillas. Selections] <u>Coleccion de Tona-</u>
      <u>dillas, escritas en estilo antiguo</u>. 11 Songs.
      International: (S, E), $2.50.

GRIEG, Edvard Hagerup, 1843-1907.
   392. [Songs. Selections] Album: 12 Songs. C. F.
      Peters: high or medium voice, $4.75 each.

HÄNDEL, Georg Friedrich, 1685-1759.
   393. [Songs. Selections] Songs from the Oratorios.
      Novello: volumes for soprano, contralto, tenor,
      baritone/bass, (G, E), $5.00 each.

HAYDN, Joseph, 1732-1809.
   394. [Songs. Selections] Canzonettas and Songs for
      Voice with Piano Accompaniment. Edited by L.
      Landshoff. C. F. Peters: high voice, (E, G),
      $4.50.

HINDEMITH, Paul, 1895-1963.
   395. [Das Marienleben (1948)] <u>Das Marien Leben</u>, 15
      Movements for Soprano and Piano. Schott:
      (E, G), $5.00 each.

IVES, Charles Edward, 1874-1954.
   396. [Songs] 114 Songs. Peer: (E), $12.95.

LISZT, Franz, 1811-1886.
   397. [Songs. Selections] 30 Songs. Dover: $4.00.

MAHLER, Gustav, 1860-1911.
Performing edition:
398. [Kindertotenlieder. Piano-vocal score] Kindertotenlieder. C. F. Peters: high or medium voice,
(G, E), $10.00 each.

Study score:
399. [Kindertotenlieder] Kindertotenlieder: für
eine Singstimme und Orchester. International:
(G, E), $2.50.

Performing edition:
400. [Lieder eines fahrenden Gesellen] Songs of a
Wayfarer (1883). International: medium voice,
(G, E), $2.50.

MOZART, Johann Chrysostom Wolfgang Amadeus, 1756-1791.
401. [Songs. Selections] Album: 29 Songs. Edited
by Friedlaender. C. F. Peters: high, medium,
or low voice, (G), $4.25 each.

402. [Songs. Selections] 21 Concert Arias for
Soprano. G. Schirmer: (orig., E), 2v., $2.50
each; $5.00 total.

MUSORGSKIĬ, Modest Petrovich, 1839-1881.
403. [The Nursery] Nursery (Song Cycle). International: (R, E), $2.50.

404. [Songs and dances of death] Songs and Dances
of Death. International: high, medium, or low
voice, (R, E), $2.50 each.

POULENC, Francis, 1899-1963.
405. [Banalités] Banalités: Cinq Melodies sur des
Poèmes de Guillaume Apollinaire. Eschig:
medium voice, (F), $5.50.

PROKOF'EV, Sergeĭ Sergeevich, 1891-1953.
406. [Le vilain petit canard] The Ugly Duckling,
for Mezzo-soprano and Orchestra. Boosey &
Hawkes: (E, F, G), $4.50.

PURCELL, Henry, 1658 or 9-1695.
407. [Songs. Selections] 20 Favourite Songs.
Galaxy: (E), $5.75.

RACHMANINOFF, Sergei, 1873-1943.
    408.   [Songs. Selections] Selected Songs for High
           or Medium Voice and Piano. Gutheil: (R, E),
           $3.50.

RAVEL, Maurice, 1875-1937.
    409.   [Don Quichotte à Dulcinée] Don Quichotte à
           Dulcinée (Baritone or Tenor) (originally for
           tenor and orchestra. Durand: (F), $2.50.

    410,   [Melodies populaires grecques] Cinq melodies
           populaires grecques (1907). 5 Greek Folk Songs.
           International: (F, G, E), $2.50.

ROREM, Ned, 1923-
    411.   [Poems of love and the rain] Poems of Love and
           the Rain for Mezzo-soprano and Piano. Boosey
           & Hawkes: (E), $4.50.

    412.   [Visits to St. Elizabeth's] Visits to St.
           Elizabeth's. Boosey & Hawkes: (E), $1.50.

SCHÖNBERG, Arnold, 1874-1951.
    413.   [Gedichte aus das Buch der hängenden Gärten]
           Book of the Hanging Gardens, Op. 15 (1907).
           Universal: high voice, (G, F), $8.00.

SCHUBERT, Franz Peter, 1797-1828.
    414.   [Die Schöne Mullerin]

    415.   [Schwanengesang]

    416.   [Songs. Selections]

    417   [Die Winterreise]

       Performing editions:
           Complete Song Cycles. Reprint of the Breitkopf
           & Hartel edition. Dover: (G, E), $4.00.

           1st Vocal Album. Four parts complete in 1 vol.
           G. Schirmer: high or low voice, (G, E), $4.00
           each.

       Study score:
           200 Songs. Edited by Sergius Kagen. Vol. 1.
           International: (G, E), $2.50.

SCHUMANN, Robert Alexander, 1810-1856.
  418. [Dichterliebe]

  419. [Frauenliebe und Leben]

  420. [Liederkreis, op. 24, op. 39]

      Performing edition:
          Vocal Album. G. Schirmer: high or low voice,
          (G, E), $4.00 each.

      Study score:
          Lieder, Vol. 1, Four Song Cycles . . . .
          Lea: (G, E), $1.50.

STRAUSS, Richard, 1864-1949.
  421. [Songs. Selections] 30 Songs. Edited by
        Sergius Kagen. International: high, medium,
        or low voice, $5,00 each.

STRAVINSKIĬ, Igor' Fedorovich, 1882-1971.
  422. [In memoriam Dylan Thomas] In Memoriam Dylan
        Thomas for Tenor, String Quartet and Four
        Trombones. Boosey & Hawkes: (E), $2.50.

  423. [Poems; arr.] Two Poems and Three Japanese
        Lyrics, for High Voice and Chamber Orchestra.
        Boosey & Hawkes: (R, F, E, G), $10.00.

THOMSON, Virgil.
  424. [Songs from William Blake] Five Songs from
        William Blake. Peer: (E), $4.00.

VAUGHAN WILLIAMS, Ralph, 1872-1958.
  425. [Mystical songs. Piano-vocal score] Five
        Mystical Songs, for Baritone Solo, Chorus and
        Orchestra. Stainer & Bell: medium voice,
        (E), $4.50.

  426. [Songs of travel] Songs of Travel, for High or
        Low Voice and Piano or Orchestra. Boosey &
        Hawkes: (E), $3.50.

VILLA-LOBOS, Heitor, 1886-1959.
  427. [Bachianas brasileiras, no. 5, soprano & string
        orchestra] Bachianas Brasileiras No. 5 for

Soprano & 8 Celli.   Associated Music Publishers:
(P, E), $2.50.

WAGNER, Richard, 1813-1883.
   428. [Gedichte von Mathilde Wesendonck] <u>Wesendonck</u>
      <u>Songs</u> (1857-8). C. F. Peters: high or low voice,
      (G, E), $4.75 each.

WEBERN, Anton von, 1883-1945.
   429. [Geistliche Lieder, wind, hapr & string
      accompaniment, op. 15] Fünf Geistliche Lieder
      for Soprano, Violin, Flute, Clarinet, Trumpet,
      Harp. Universal: (G), $7.00.

   430. [Lieder, op. 12] Vier Lieder, für Gesang und
      Klavier. Universal: (G), $4.25.

   431. [Lieder, op. 23] Drei Gesänge. Universal:
      medium voice, $3.75.

   432. [Lieder, op. 25] Drei Lieder, Op. 25. Univer-
      sal: (G), $3.75.

WOLF, Hugo, 1860-1903.
   433. [Songs. Selections] 65 Songs. Edited by
      Sergius Kagen. International: high or low
      voice, (G, E), $7.50 each.

ANTHOLOGIES

   434. <u>Alte Meister des Deutschen Liedes</u>. Edited by
      Hans J. Moser. C. F. Peters: medium voice,
      (G), $6.00.

   435. <u>Anthology of Italian Song of the 17th and 18th</u>
      <u>Centuries</u>. Edited by A. Parisotti. G. Schirmer:
      high, medium, or low voice, (I, E), 2v., $2.75
      each; $5.50 total for each voice range.

   436. <u>Contemporary Art Song Album</u>. Galaxy: Book 1
      (high), $2.50; Book 2 (medium), $3.00.

   437. <u>Contemporary Songs in English</u>. Carl Fischer:
      medium-high or medium-low voice, $5.00 each.

438. 40 French Songs. Edited by Julius Kagen. Inter-
      national: high, medium, or low voice, 2v.,
      $5.00 each; $10.00 total for each voice range.

439. 40 Songs from Elizabethan and Jacobean
      Songbooks. Edited by Edmund Fellowes.
      Stainer & Bell: high or low voice, 4 books,
      $2.50 each; $10.00 total for each voice range.

440. Music of the Moravians in America. No. 1:
      Ten Sacred Songs for Soprano, Strings and
      Organ. Edited by Hans T. David. C. F. Peters:
      (G, E), $4.50.

441. Songs by 22 Americans. G. Schirmer: $5.00.

442. Spanish Songs of the 18th Century. Edited by
      Juan Subira. International: $5.00.

ARIA COLLECTIONS

443. Aria Albums . . . Famous Arias from Cantatas,
      Oratorios, and Operas. C. F. Peters: (orig.,
      G), 5v. Soprano, $9.50; mezzo-soprano, $7.50;
      alto, $8.50; tenor, $8.50; baritone/bass, $12.00.

444. Operatic Anthology: Celebrated Arias Selected
      from Operas by Old and Modern Composers. Edited
      by Kurt Adler. 5 v. G. Schirmer: volumes for
      soprano, mezzo-soprano, and alto, tenor, bari-
      tone, bass. $7.00 each; $35.00 total.

FOLK SONG COLLECTIONS

445. Boni, Margaret Bradford. Fireside Book of
      Folk Songs. Simon & Schuster: $14.95.

446. Canteloube, Joseph, ed. Chants d'Auverne. 5 v.
      Heugel: $5.00 each; $25.00 total.

447. Downes, Olin. Treasury of American Song.
      2d rev. ed. Alfred A. Knopf: $15.00.

448. Lomax, Alan. The Folk Songs of North America.
      Doubleday: $14.95; paper, $6.95. See also
      AMERICAN MUSIC: Books.

PIANO-VOCAL SCORES:
OPERAS, ORATORIOS, ETC.

A piano-vocal score is one in which the instrumental parts are condensed for performance on a keyboard instrument, resulting in greater prominence
of the vocal parts. They are designed for vocal
performers, but also provide useful means for
following performances. In 1978 the approximate cost
of this entire list was $593.35 in paper and $892.00
cloth-bound preferred. Many of the piano-vocal scores
are not available in cloth-bound edition at all.

OPERAS

BARTÓK, Béla, 1881-1945.
   449. [Duke Bluebeard's Castle. Piano-vocal score.
         English] Bluebeard's Castle (1911). Boosey
         & Hawkes: $35.00.

BEETHOVEN, Ludwig van, 1770-1827.
   450. Fidelio. Piano-vocal score. English & German]
         Fidelio, Op. 72. Boosey & Hawkes: $13.00.
         Kalmus: $7.50. G. Schirmer: $6.95; $15.00,
         cloth.

BELLINI, Vincenzo, 1805-1835.
   451. [Norma. Piano-vocal score. English & Italian]
         Norma (1831). Boosey & Hawkes: $7.50. Kalmus:
         $7.50. G. Schirmer: $6.95; $15.00, cloth.

BERG, Alban, 1883-1935.
   452. [Wozzeck. Piano-vocal score. German] Wozzeck
         (1914-21). Universal: $35.00.

BERLIOZ, Hector, 1803-1869.
   453. [La damnation de Faust. Piano-vocal score.
         English & French] La Damnation de Faust, Op. 24.
         Kalmus: $7.50.

BIZET, Georges, 1838-1875.
    454. [Carmen. Piano-vocal score. English &
          French] Carmen (1875). Boosey & Hawkes:
          $7.50. Kalmus: $7.50. G. Schirmer: $6.95;
          $15.00, cloth.

BRITTEN, Benjamin, 1913-
    455. [Albert Herring. Piano-vocal score. English]
          Albert Herring (1947). Boosey & Hawkes: $40.00.

CHAĬKOVSKIĬ, Petr Il'ich, 1840-1893.
    456. [Eugenii Onegin. Piano-vocal score. English
          & Russian] Eugen Onegin, Op. 24. Kalmus:
          $7.50. G. Schirmer: $15.00, cloth.

DONIZETTI, Gaetano, 1797-1848.
    457. [Lucia di Lammermoor. Piano-vocal score.
          English & Italian] Lucia di Lammermoor (1835).
          Kalmus: $7.50. G. Schirmer: $6.95; $15.00, cloth.

GILBERT and SULLIVAN. See Sullivan, Sir Arthur Seymour

GLUCK, Christoph Willibald, Ritter von, 1714-1787.
    458. [Orfeo ed Euridice. Piano-vocal score. Eng-
          lish & Italian] Orfeo ed Euridice. Kalmus:
          $5.00. G. Schirmer: $11.50, cloth.

GOUNOD, Charles François, 1818-1893.
    459. [Faust. Piano-vocal score. English & French]
          Faust (1859). Kalmus: $7.50. G. Schirmer:
          $6.95; $15.00, cloth.

HUMPERDINCK, Engelbert, 1854-1921.
    460. [Hansel und Gretel. Piano-vocal score. English]
          Hansel and Gretel. Kalmus: $6.00. G. Schirmer:
          $6.95; $11.50, cloth. (NB: no English and
          German editions are available at this time.)

LEONCAVALLO, Ruggiero, 1858-1919.
    461. [I Pagliacci. Piano-vocal score. English &
          Italian] Pagliacci (1892). Kalmus: $7.50.
          G. Schirmer: $6.95; $15.00, cloth.

MASCAGNI, Pietro, 1863-1945.
    462. [Cavalleria rusticana. Piano-vocal score. Eng-
          lish & Italian] Cavalleria Rusticana (1889).
          Kalmus: $7.50. G. Schirmer: $6.95; $11.50, cloth.

MASSENET, Jules Émile Frédéric, 1842-1912.
  463. [Manon. Piano-vocal score. English &
       French] Manon. Kalmus: $7.50. G. Schirmer:
       $6.95; $15.00, cloth.

MENOTTI, Gian Carlo, 1911-
  464. [Amahl and the night visitors. Piano-vocal
       score. English] Amahl and the Night Visitors
       (1951). G. Schirmer: $7.50, cloth.

MONTEVERDI, Claudio, 1567-1643.
  465. [L'Orfeo. Piano-vocal score. English &
       Italian] L'Orfeo. Boosey & Hawkes: $30.00.
       Broude Brothers: $15.00.

MOZART, Johann Chrysostom Wolfgang Amadeus, 1756-1791.
  466. [Cosi fan tutti. Piano-vocal score. English
       & Italian] Cosi Fan Tutti, K. 588 (1790).
       Boosey & Hawkes: $15.00. Kalmus: $7.50. G.
       Schirmer: $6.95; $15.00, cloth.

  467. [Don Giovanni. Piano-vocal score. English &
       Italian] Don Giovanni, K. 527 (1787). Boosey
       & Hawkes: $10.00; $15.00, cloth. Kalmus:
       $7.50, G. Schirmer: $6.95; $15.00, cloth.

  468. [Le nozze di Figaro. Piano-vocal score. Eng-
       lish & Italian] Marriage of Figaro, K. 492
       (1786). Boosey & Hawkes: $10.00. Kalmus:
       $7.50. G. Schirmer: $6.95; $15.00, cloth.

  469. [Die Zauberflöte. Piano-vocal score. English
       & German] Magic Flute, K. 620 (1791). Boosey
       & Hawkes: $10.00; $15.00, cloth. Kalmus:
       $7.50. G. Schirmer: $6.95; $15.00, cloth.

MUSORGSKIĬ, Modest Petrovich, 1839-1881.
  470. [Boris Godunov. Piano-vocal score. English &
       German] Boris Godounov (1874). Kalmus: $9.00.
       (NB: no English & Russian edition available at
       this time.)

OFFENBACH, Jacques, 1819-1880.
  471. [Les contes d'Hoffmann. Piano-vocal score.
       English & French] The Tales of Hoffmann.
       Kalmus: $7.50. G. Schirmer: $6.95; $15.00,
       cloth.

PUCCINI, Giacomo, 1858-1924.
472. [La Bohème. Piano-vocal score. English &
Italian] La Bohème (1896). Kalmus: $7.50.
G. Schirmer: $6.95; $15.00, cloth.

473. [Madama Butterfly. Piano-vocal score. English
& Italian] Madame Butterfly (1904). Kalmus:
$7.50. G. Schirmer: $6.95; $15.00, cloth.

474. [Tosca. Piano-vocal score. English & Italian]
Tosca (1900). Kalmus: $7.50. G. Schirmer:
$6.95; $15.00, cloth.

PURCELL, Henry, 1658 or 9-1695.
475. [Dido and Aeneas. Piano-vocal score. English]
Dido and Aeneas. Boosey & Hawkes: $15.00.
Kalmus: $3.00.

ROSSINI, Gioacchino Antonio, 1792-1868.
476. [Il barbiere di Siviglia. Piano-vocal score.
English & Italian] The Barber of Seville (1816).
Boosey & Hawkes: $7.50. Kalmus: $7.50. G.
Schirmer: $6.95; $15.00, cloth.

SMETANA, Bedřich, 1824-1884.
477. [Prodaná nevěsta. Piano-vocal score. English]
The Bartered Bride. Boosey & Hawkes: $7.50.
G. Schirmer: $6.95; $15.00, cloth.

STRAUSS, Johann, 1825-1899.
478. [Die Fledermaus. Piano-vocal score. English
& German] Die Fledermaus. Boosey & Hawkes:
$7.50. Kalmus: $7.50. G. Schirmer: $7.50.

STRAUSS, RICHARD, 1864-1949.
479. [Der Rosenkavalier. Piano-vocal score. English
& German] Der Rosenkavalier, Op. 59 (1910).
Boosey & Hawkes: $38.00.

480. [Salome. Piano-vocal score. English & German]
Salome, Op. 54 (1904-05). Boosey & Hawkes:
$10.00. Kalmus: $6.00.

STRAVINSKIĬ, Igor' Fedorovich, 1882-1971.
481. [The Rake's Progress. Piano-vocal score.
English] The Rake's Progress (1951). Boosey
& Hawkes: $30.00.

SULLIVAN, Sir Arthur Seymour, 1842-1900.
   482. [H.M.S. Pinafore. Piano-vocal score. English]
       Pinafore. Kalmus: $4.50. G. Schirmer: $4.50.

   483. [Mikado. Piano-vocal score. English] Mikado.
       Kalmus: $5.00. G. Schirmer: $6.00.

   484. [The pirates of Penzance. Piano-vocal score.
       English] Pirates of Penzance. Kalmus: $5.00.
       G. Schirmer: $5.00.

VERDI, Giuseppe, 1813-1901.
   485. [Aida. Piano-vocal score. English & Italian]
       Aida (1871). Kalmus: $7.50. G. Schirmer:
       $6.95; $15.00, cloth.

   486. [Un ballo in maschera. Piano-vocal score.
       English & Italian] The Masked Ball (1859).
       Boosey & Hawkes: $7.50. Kalmus: $7.50. G.
       Schirmer: $6.95; $15.00, cloth.

   487. [Otello. Piano-vocal score. English & Italian]
       Otello (1887). Kalmus: $7.50. G. Schirmer:
       $6.95; $15.00, cloth.

   488. [Rigoletto. Piano-vocal score. English &
       Italian] Rigoletto (1851). Boosey & Hawkes:
       $7.50. Kalmus: $7.50. G. Schirmer: $6.95;
       $15.00, cloth.

   489. [La Traviata. Piano-vocal score. English &
       Italian] La Traviata (1853). Boosey & Hawkes:
       $7.50. G. Schirmer: $6.95; $15.00, cloth.

   490. [Il trovatore. Piano-vocal score. English &
       Italian] Il Trovatore (1853). Boosey & Hawkes:
       $12.00. Kalmus: $7.50. G. Schirmer: $6.95;
       $15.00, cloth.

WAGNER, Richard, 1813-1883.
   491. [Lohengrin. Piano-vocal score. English &
       German] Lohengrin (1850). Kalmus: $7.50.
       G. Schirmer: $6.95; $15.00, cloth.

492.   [Die Meistersinger von Nürnberg. Piano-vocal
       score. English & German] Die Meistersinger
       von Nürnberg (1868). Kalmus: $8.00. G.
       Schirmer: $6.95; $15.00, cloth.

493.   [Der Ring des Nibelungen. Gotterdämmerung.
       Piano-vocal score. English & German] Gotter-
       dämmerung (1876). Kalmus: $7.50. G. Schirmer:
       $6.95; $15.00, cloth.

494.   [Der Ring des Nibelungen. Das Rheingold.
       Piano-vocal score. English & German] Das
       Rheingold (1869). Kalmus: $7.50. G. Schirmer:
       $6.95; $15.00, cloth.

495.   [Der Ring des Nibelungen. Siegfried. Piano-
       vocal score. English & German] Siegfried
       (1876). Kalmus: $7.50. G. Schirmer: $6.95;
       $15.00, cloth.

496.   [Der Ring des Nibelungen. Die Walküre. Piano-
       vocal score. English & German] Die Walküre
       (1870). Kalmus: $7.50. G. Schirmer: $6.95;
       $15.00, cloth.

497.   [Tristan und Isolde. Piano-vocal score. Eng-
       lish & German] Tristan und Isolde (1865).
       Kalmus: $7.50. G. Schirmer: $6.95; $15.00,
       cloth.

WEILL, Kurt, 1900-1950.
496.   [Die Dreigroschenoper. Piano-vocal score.
       German] Three Penny Opera (1928). Universal:
       $15.00.

CANTATAS, MASSES, ORATORIOS, ETC.

BACH, Johann Sebastian, 1685-1750.
499.   [Christ lag in Todesbanden, S. 4. Piano-vocal
       score. English & German] Cantatas. No. 4.
       Christ lag in Todesbanden. Kalmus: $1.25.
       G. Schirmer: $1.75.

500.   [Jauchzet Gott in allen Landen, S. 51. Piano-
       vocal score. English & German] Cantatas. No.
       51. Jauchzet Gott in allen Landen. Breitkopf
       & Härtel: $3.25.

501. [Johannespassion. Piano-vocal score. English
& German] St. John Passion, S. 245. Kalmus:
$5.00.

502. [Magnificat, S. 243, D major. Piano-vocal
score. Latin] Magnificat in D, S. 243.
Kalmus: $1.25. C. F. Peters: $2.00. G.
Schirmer: $2.00.

503. [Mass, S. 232, B. minor. Piano-vocal score.
Latin] Mass in b, S. 232. Kalmus: $3.50.
C. F. Peters: $5.50. G. Schirmer: $5.00;
$7.50, cloth.

504. [Matthäuspassion. Piano-vocal score. English
and German] St. Matthew Passion, S. 244.
Kalmus: $4.50. C. F. Peters: $5.50.

505. [Wachet auf, ruft uns die Stimme, S. 140.
Piano-vocal score. English & German] Cantatas.
No. 140, Wachet auf! Kalmus: $1.25. G.
Schirmer: $1.25.

506. [Weichet nur, betrübte Schatten, S. 202. Piano-
vocal score. German] Cantatas. No. 202,
Weichet nur (Wedding Cantata). Breitkopf &
Härtel: $3.25. Kalmus: $1.50. C. F. Peters:
$7.50.

507. [Weihnachts-Oratorium. Piano-vocal score.
English and German] Christmas Oratorio,
S. 248. Kalmus: $2.50.

BEETHOVEN, Ludwig van, 1770-1827.
508. [Mass, op. 123, D major. Piano-vocal score.
Latin] Missa Solemnis in D, Op. 123. Kalmus:
$2.50. C. F. Peters: $5.50. G. Schirmer: $4.00.

BERLIOZ, Hector, 1803-1869.
509. [Requiem. Piano-vocal score. Latin] Requiem,
Op. 5. (Grande Messe des Morts). Kalmus:
$2.00. G. Schirmer: $3.50.

BLOCH, Ernest, 1880-1959.
510. ['Avodat ha-kodish. Piano-vocal score. English
& Hebrew] Sacred Service, Avodat Hakodish
(1930-1933). Broude Brothers: $4.75.

BRAHMS,   Johannes, 1833-1897.
  511. [Ein deutsches Requiem. Piano-vocal score.
        German] German Requiem, Op. 45. Kalmus:
        $1.50. C. F. Peters: $3.50. G. Schirmer:
        $2.50.

BRITTEN, Benjamin, 1913-
  512. [A ceremony of carols. Piano-vocal score.
        English] Ceremony of Carols, Op. 28 (1912).
        Boosey & Hawkes: $2.00.

BYRD, William, 1542 or 3-1623.
  513. [Mass. 4 voices] Mass in 4 parts. Stainer
        & Bell: $2.25.

FAURÉ, Gabriel Urbain, 1845-1924.
  514. [Requiem. Piano-vocal score. English and
        Latin] Requiem, Op. 48 (1887). Kalmus:
        $1.75. G. Schirmer: $2.00.

GUILLAUME de Machaut, d. 1377.
  515. [La messe de Nostre Dame] Machaut, Guillaume
        de. Mass: Notre Dame. Oxford University.
        Press: $3.75.

HÄNDEL, Georg Friedrich, 1685-1759.
  516. [Messiah. Piano-vocal score. English]
        Messiah (oratorio). Kalmus: $2.50. C. F.
        Peters: $5.50. G. Schirmer: $4.95; $15.00,
        cloth.

HAYDN, Joseph, 1732-1809.
  517. [Mass, H. XXII, 11, D minor. Piano-vocal
        score. Latin] Mass No. 9 in d, Missa
        Solemnis (Nelson Mass). Kalmus: $1.50. C. F.
        Peters: $4.50. G. Schirmer: $2.00.

  518. [Die Schöpfung. Piano-vocal score. English &
        German] Creation (oratorio). Kalmus: $2.00.
        C. F. Peters: $5.50. G. Schirmer: $5.00;
        $7.50, cloth.

HONEGGER, Arthur, 1892-1955.
  519. [Le roi David. Piano-vocal score. English &
        French] Roi David (1921). E. C. Schirmer
        (Foetisch): $15.00.

MENDELSSOHN-BARTHOLDY, Felix, 1809-1847.
520.   [Elias. Piano-vocal score. English & German]
       Elijah, Op. 70 (oratorio). Kalmus: $2.50.
       C. F. Peters: $10.50. G. Schirmer: $4.00;
       $5.00, cloth.

MOZART, Johann Chrysostom Wolfgang Amadeus, 1756-1791.
521.   [Exultate jubilate. Piano-vocal score. Latin]
       Exultate Jubilate, K. 165. Breitkopf & Härtel:
       $1.50. International: $2.00. Kalmus: $1.25.

522.   [Requiem. Piano-vocal score] Requiem, K. 626.
       Kalmus: $1.75. C. F. Peters: $3.00. G.
       Schirmer: $2.25.

PALESTRINA, Giovanni Pierluigi da, 1525?-1594.
523.   [Missa Papae Marcelli] Missa Papae Marcelli.
       Associated Music Publishers: $1.00. Kalmus:
       $2.00. G. Schirmer: $3.50.

PERGOLESI, Giovanni Battista, 1710-1736.
524.   [Stabat Mater. Piano-vocal score. Latin]
       Stabat Mater. Kalmus: $1.50. C. F. Peters:
       $5.50. G. Schirmer: $2.00.

SCHUBERT, Franz Peter, 1797-1828.
525.   [Mass, D. 167, G major. Piano-vocal score.
       Latin] Mass No. 2 in G, D. 167. Kalmus:
       $1.50. C. F. Peters: $5.00. G. Schirmer:
       $2.00.

SCHÜTZ, Heinrich, 1585-1672.
526.   [Historia von der Geburt Jesu Christi. Piano-
       vocal score. English & German] Christmas
       Oratorio. Kalmus: $2.50.

STRAVINSKIĬ, Igor' Fedorovich, 1882-
527.   [Symphonie des Psaumes. Piano-vocal score.
       Latin] Symphony of Psalms (1930). Boosey &
       Hawkes: $2.00. Kalmus: $1.50.

VAUGHAN WILLIAMS, Ralph, 1872-1958.
528.   [This day. Piano-vocal score. English] Hodie.
       A Christmas Cantata. Oxford University Press:
       $4.50.

VERDI, Giuseppe, 1813-1901.
   529. [Requiem. Piano-vocal score] <u>Requiem Mass,</u>
        <u>in Memory of Manzoni</u> (1874). Kalmus: $2.00.
        C. F. Peters: $4.50. G. Schirmer: $4.00.

VIVALDI, Antonio, 1680(ca.)-1741.
   530. [Gloria, 4 mixed voices & orchestra. Piano-
        vocal score. English & Latin] Gloria in D.
        Kalmus: $2.00. G. Schirmer: $2.50.

MUSIC LITERATURE:
REFERENCE BOOKS

    This list of basic music reference books is di-
rected toward the librarian who is not a music
specialist, serving a clientele in a public, school, or
a small college library, and to the reader who is
interested in a brief guide to reference sources in
English. It is intended to assist this librarian and
reader in making appropriate choices for their needs.
Both paperback and clothbound trade editions are cited.
The annotations offer an indication of the scope, content and special features of each work. The ten titles
marked with an asterisk (*) might be considered as core
works in a collection of music reference books. In
1978 the total approximate cost of books on this list
was $2191.00, clothbound preferred (including $1000.00
for the New Grove Dictionary, 6th ed.), and $1200.00,
paperback preferred (including $79.50 for Grove's
Dictionary, 5th ed.) The ten core titles totaled
$1215.00, clothbound preferred, and $295.00, paperback
preferred.

    The comprehensive bibliographies of reference
sources, which may be consulted for further information,
are Vincent Duckles' Music Reference and Research
Materials: An Annotated Bibliography, 3rd ed., New York:
The Free Press, 1974, $10.95 and Guy Marco's Information
on Music: A Handbook of Reference Sources in European
Languages, v. 1- , Littleton, CO: Libraries Unlimited,
1975-   , v.1: $11.50. Neither of these prices has
been included in the total given above.

DICTIONARIES AND ENCYCLOPEDIAS

General

531. Blom, Eric, comp. Everyman's Dictionary of
      Music. Revised by Jack Westrup. New York: St.
      Martin's Press, Inc., 1972. $15.00. Paper,
      New American Library, $4.95.

      A surprisingly comprehensive pocket-sized diction-
      ary written with the student in mind. Includes
      good biographies (English emphasis) and illus-
      trations.

532. *The New Grove Dictionary of Music and Musicians.
      Edited by Stanley Sadie. 6th ed. London: Mac-
      millan Press, 1979. 20v. $1000.00. (5th ed.
      New York: St. Martin's Press, Inc., 1954. 10v.
      Paper, $79.50.)

      Largest English language music encyclopedia. An
      excellent guide to the lives and works of com-
      posers, for broad scope articles (i.e., "Ornamen-
      tation," "Bagpipe," "German music," etc.) and for
      musical definitions.

533. Scholes, Percy A. The Oxford Companion to Music.
      10th ed. London: Oxford University Press, 1970.
      $27.50.

      The OCM covers large and small topics in concise
      format and curt British style. It is designed
      for the sophisticated amateur.

534. Thompson, Oscar, ed. International Cyclopedia of
      Music and Musicians. 10th ed. New York: Dodd,
      Mead & Co., 1975. $49.95.

      An excellent one-volume dictionary which offers
      essential information in a popular style. It is
      filled with obscure musicians and esoteric terms
      but is good reading. It is also a good source
      for musical societies and organizations.

Special Topics

535. Anderson, Ruth E. <u>Contemporary American Com-</u>
      <u>posers: A Biographical Dictionary</u>. Boston:
      G. K. Hall, 1976. $50.00.

      Career data, selected works, and current position
      and address for more than 4,000 composers. A
      separate list of women composers is appended.

536. *Apel, Willi. <u>Harvard Dictionary of Music</u>. 2nd
      ed. Cambridge, MA: Harvard University Press,
      1969. $20.00.

      The most scholarly single-volume musical dic-
      tionary in English. It contains brief definitions
      and larger essays on topics other than bio-
      graphical.

537. Cobbett, W. W. <u>Cobbett's Cyclopedic Survey of</u>
      <u>Chamber Music</u>. London: Oxford University Press,
      1929. 3v. (Vol. 3 is supplement, 1963). $48.00.

      Written in a leisurely and personal style, this
      is a very complete guide to works for three to
      nine solo instruments and non-piano duets. It
      explains musical as well as historical features
      of each work.

538. Davidson, James Robert. <u>A Dictionary of Protestant</u>
      <u>Church Music</u>. Metuchen, NJ: The Scarecrow Press,
      1975. $7.50.

      Definitions of terms and longer essays covering
      music and musical traditions of non-Catholic
      Western churches are combined.

539. Feather, Leonard. <u>The Encyclopedia of Jazz</u>. New
      York: Horizon Press, 1960. $17.50.

540. _____ . <u>Encyclopedia of Jazz in the Sixties</u>.
      New York: Horizon Press, 1967. $17.50.

541. _____ and Ira Gitler. <u>The Encyclopedia of</u>
      <u>Jazz in the Seventies</u>. New York: Horizon Press,
      1976. $20.00.

Together these volumes make up the most comprehensive source for identifying past and current
jazz performers, critics and composers. Illus-
trations, special lists, discographies and bib-
liographies supplement each volume.

542.   Gold, Robert. Jazz Talk: A Dictionary of the
       Colorful Language that has Emerged from America's
       Own Music. Indianapolis: Bobbs-Merrill Co., Inc.,
       1975. $10.00; paper, $5.95.

       A dictionary of jazz terms and slang based on
       historical usage. Sociologists as well as
       musicians find this a useful and interesting
       source.

543.   Green, Stanley. Encyclopedia of the Musical
       Theatre. New York: Dodd, Mead & Co., 1976. $17.50.

       Performers, choreographers, directors, composers,
       and lyricists plus shows and songs are given
       comprehensive coverage. Some useful appendices
       such as long-run shows and award winners are
       added.

544.   The International Who's Who in Music and Musicians'
       Directory. Edited by Adrian Gaster. 8th ed.
       Detroit: Gale Research Company, 1977. $59.50.

       Contains 10,000 biographical entries, with emphasis
       on classical music and appendices listing the
       world's orchestras, music conservatories,
       libraries, and competitions.

545.   Julian, John. Dictionary of Hymnology. 2nd rev.
       ed. New York: Dover, 1957 (repr. of 1907 ed.).
       $17.50.

       The standard reference source contains an enormous
       amount of information on both musical and literary
       aspects of Christian hymnody.

546.   Marcuse, Sibyl. Musical Instruments: A Compre-
       hensive Dictionary. New York: W. W. Norton & Co.,
       Inc., 1975. (repr. of 1964 ed.). Paper, $6.95.

Describes Western and non-Western instruments
with definitions of related terms, from anti-
quity to the present.

547. Musical Instruments of the World: An Illustrated
      Encyclopedia. Edited by the Diagram Group.
      New York: Two Continents/Paddington Press, 1976.
      $16.95.

      Thousands of instruments, Western, Eastern, and
      folk, are illustrated with superb drawings and
      are fully identified. Playing positions and
      how they work are usually also shown.

548. Orrey, Leslie, and Gilbert Chase, eds. The
      Encyclopedia of Opera. New York: Charles
      Scribner's Sons, 1976. $22.50.

      A well-illustrated dictionary of people, places,
      and opera. Musical comedies are included.

549. Rich, Maria F., ed. Who's Who in Opera. New
      York: Arno Press, 1976. $65.00.

      An international biographical directory of people
      currently associated with opera. Includes pro-
      files of 101 opera companies.

550. Shestack, Melvin. The Country Music Encyclopedia.
      New York: Thomas Y. Crowell Co., 1974. $13.95.

      Basic biographical and career facts about several
      hundred country music personalities. Well-
      illustrated; includes music for several song
      classics and lengthy discography.

551. *Slonimsky, Nicolas, ed. Baker's Biographical
      Dictionary of Musicians. 5th ed. New York:
      G. Schirmer, 1958. With 1971 supplement. $35.00.
      Suppl. only, $7.50.

      This 2,000 page work is the most comprehensive
      source for identifying musicians of all times
      and places. It covers popular and folk musicians
      as well as musicologists, classical composers and
      performers, describing their careers, notable
      works, and achievements.

552.   Stambler, Irwin. <u>The Encyclopedia of Pop, Rock,</u>
        <u>and Soul</u>. New York: St. Martin's Press, Inc.,
        1974. $19.95.

        Traces careers of performing groups and individuals,
        describes important events in the pop musical
        scene and defines pop music related terms.
        Arranged in a single alphabet.

553.   Thompson, Kenneth. <u>A Dictionary of Twentieth</u>
        <u>Century Composers (1911-1971)</u>. New York: St.
        Martin's Press, Inc., 1973. $30.00.

        A comprehensive list of the musical and literary
        works of, and selected literature about, thirty-
        two reknowned but deceased composers who lived in
        this century.

554.   *Vinton, John. <u>Dictionary of Contemporary Music</u>.
        New York: E. P. Dutton, 1974. $25.00.

        Terms, musical genre, instruments, trends and
        people associated with twentieth-century music
        are treated comprehensively.

INDEXES, BIBLIOGRAPHIES AND DISCOGRAPHIES

555.   Barlow, Harold, and Sam Morgenstern, eds. <u>A Dic-</u>
        <u>tionary of Musical Themes</u>. Rev. ed. New York:
        Crown Publishers, Inc., 1975. $8.95.

556.   _____. <u>A Dictionary of Opera and Song Themes</u>:
        <u>Including Cantatas, Oratorios, Lieder, and Art</u>
        <u>Songs</u>. Rev. ed. New York: Crown Publishers,
        Inc., 1976. $9.95.

        This classic source lists in musical notation,
        themes from the standard instrumental and vocal
        literature respectively. Both volumes are indexed
        with a unique notational code.

557.   *Berkowitz, Freda Pastor. <u>Popular Titles and Sub-</u>
        <u>titles of Musical Compositions</u>. 2nd ed. Metuchen,
        NJ: The Scarecrow Press, 1975. $8.00.

Nicknames and subtitles of well-known and
obscure musical works are identified with refer-
ences to the originals.

558.   *Charles, Sydney Robinson. A Handbook of Music
       and Music Literature in Sets and Series. New
       York: The Free Press, 1972. $13.95

       A list of the contents of musical monuments,
       collected editions and series, as well as books
       and periodicals published as series.

559.   Cooper, David Edwin. International Bibliography
       of Discographies: Classical Music, Jazz and
       Blues, 1962-1972. Littleton, CO: Libraries Un-
       limited, 1975. $13.50.

       Includes buyers guides, chronologies, plus sub-
       jects and genres in its listing. "Bibliographies,
       annual cumulation" in issues of the Association
       of Recorded Sound Collections, Journal supple-
       ments this huge work.

560.   De Charms, Desiree and Paul F. Breed. Songs in
       Collections: An Index. Detroit: Information
       Coordinators, Inc., 1966. $38.00; paper, $11.00.

       Over 400 collections published between 1940 and
       1957 are listed and indexed in this up-dating of
       Sears.

561.   Gray, Michael H. and Gerald D. Gibson. Biblio-
       graphy of Discographies: Classical Music, 1925-
       1975. Vol. 1. New York: R. R. Bowker Company,
       1977. $15.95.

       The first of five volumes devoted to discographies
       in all subject areas. The projected series
       includes jazz, popular music, ethnic and folk
       music, and general discographies of music, speech,
       animal sounds, etc.

562.   Havlice, Patricia Pate. Popular Song Index. Metu-
       chen, NJ: The Scarecrow Press, 1975. $30.00.

More than 300 song anthologies of pop, rock, hymns,
folk and topical songs are indexed by title, first
line, chorus, composer, and lyricist. Some Renais-
sance part-songs are also included.

563.   Haywood, Charles. Bibliography of North American
       Folklore and Folksong. 2v. New York: Dover, 1961.
       (repr. of 1951 ed.). $30.00

       Volume 1 covers non-Indian Americans; volume 2
       covers American Indians. Each volume is sub-
       divided by regions, ethnic, occupational and
       cultural groups.

564.   Horn, David. The Literature of American Music
       in Books and Folk Music Collections: A Fully
       Annotated Bibliography. Metuchen, NJ: The
       Scarecrow Press, 1977. $20.00.

       A compilation of 1,600 items covering all aspects
       of the American musical heritage, from American
       Indian and Black music to folk, pop, and jazz.
       It includes a large section devoted to the last
       three centuries of American art music.

565.   Lewine, Richard and Alfred Simon. Songs of the
       American Theater; A Comprehensive Listing of
       More than 12,000 Songs, Including Selected Titles
       from Film and Television Productions. New York:
       Dodd, Mead & Co., 1973. $15.00.

       The list of productions and their songs, a chron-
       ology of productions 1925-1971, plus the alpha-
       betical listing of songs from shows make this the
       complete guide.

566.   *Music Index. Detroit: Information Coordinators,
       Inc., 1949-   . $55.00/year.

       Monthly with annual cumulations. A subject-author
       guide to over 300 current music periodicals from
       the United States, England, Canada, and Australia,
       and 19 non-English language countries. This is
       the primary index for music journals but does not
       include more general periodicals having articles
       on musical topics.

567. Parsons, Denys. The Directory of Tunes and
      Musical Themes. Cambridge, England: Spencer
      Brown, 1975. $15.00.

      About 15,000 vocal and instrumental themes are
      arranged by whether the succeeding notes repeat,
      ascend, or descend. Separate classical, popular,
      and national anthems categories.

568. RILM Abstracts of Musical Literature. Inter-
      national Repertory of Music Literature. New York:
      International RILM Center, v. 1, 1967-   .
      $36.00/year.

      An international quarterly journal which provides
      abstracts of current literature on music. With
      annual and five-year cumulative indexes.

569. *Schwann Record & Tape Guide. Boston: W. Schwann,
      Inc., v. 1, 1949-   . $20.00/year.

      The standard listing of currently available LP
      records, cassette and cartridge tapes which can
      be purchased through retail record and tape
      dealers. Subscriptions include Schwann-1 and
      Schwann-2.

      Schwann-1. Monthly. Entries are under composer
      with separate sections for new listing, electronic
      music, collections, musicals, current popular,
      and jazz.

      Schwann-2. Semiannual. Presents recordings in
      categories such as religious, spoken, domestic
      popular more than two years old, international
      folk and pop, classical on lesser-known labels,
      monophonic, and electronic stereo.

      Schwann Artist Issue. Irregular. 1976, $4.50.
      Entries are listed by performers, orchestras,
      chamber groups, conductors, instrumental and vocal
      soloists, choral groups, operatic groups.

HANDBOOKS AND GUIDES

570.   Brody, Elaine and Claire Brook. <u>The Music Guide
       to Great Britain</u>. New York: Dodd, Mead & Co.,
       1976. $10.00.

571.   _____. <u>The Music Guide to Austria and Germany</u>.
       New York: Dodd, Mead & Co., 1976. $10.00.

572.   _____. <u>The Music Guide to Belgium, Luxembourg,
       Holland, and Switzerland</u>. New York: Dodd, Mead
       & Co., 1977. $10.00

573.   _____. <u>The Music Guide to Italy</u>. New York:
       Dodd, Mead & Co., 1978. $10.00.

       Concert halls, opera houses, libraries, museums,
       schools, organizations, businesses, musical land-
       marks, and other music aspects of the major cities
       in each country are cited with full explanatory
       remarks, addresses, and phone numbers.

574.   Fuld, James J. <u>The Book of World-Famous Music</u>:
       <u>Classical, Popular and Folk</u>. Rev. and enl. ed.
       New York: Crown Publishers, Inc., 1971. $15.00.

       A bit of the music and a wealth of information
       (historical, biographical, bibliographical,
       anecdotal) is given for almost 1,000 well-known
       melodies.

575.   Hinson, Maurice. <u>Guide to the Pianists' Repertoire</u>.
       Edited by Irwin Freundlich. Bloomington: Indiana
       University Press, 1973. $17.50.

       Hinson's huge volume describes repertoire, notes
       difficulty, analyses hundreds of works and
       includes several useful off-beat appendices.

576.   *<u>Kobbé's Complete Opera Book</u>. Revised and edited
       by the Earl of Harewood. New York: G. P. Putnam's
       Sons, 1972. $12.95.

       This is a well-written and up-to-date source for
       background, commentary, and plots of almost all
       operas in the standard repertoire.

577. Lichtenwanger, William, comp. A Survey of Musical Instrument Collections in the United States and Canada. Ann Arbor, MI: Music Library Association, 1974. $8.50.

The entries are arranged geographically and indicate the name and address of the owner, brief description, bibliography or discography, existence of a catalog, means of access to the collection, etc.

578. Marcuse, Sibyl. A Survey of Music Instruments. New York: Harper & Row, 1975. $20.00.

A scholarly description of instruments and their families arranged by the Hornbostel Classification.

579. *Pavlakis, Christopher. The American Music Handbook. New York: The Free Press, 1974. $25.00.

Detailed information about American musical organizations, performing groups, composers and musicians, festivals, contests, periodicals and the industry is given in lists and narrative format.

580. Sandberg, Larry, and Dick Weissman. Folk Musical Sourcebook. New York: Alfred A. Knopf, Inc., 1976. $15.00; paper, $8.95.

Excellent source for lists of folk festivals, archives, periodicals about folk music, recordings, books and instructional materials as well as brief articles on folk and folk-based music of North America. At least half the book deals with recordings.

581. Shemel, Sidney M. and William Krasilousky. This Business of Music. Rev. and enl. ed. New York: Billboard Publications, 1977. $16.95.

582. _____. More About This Business of Music. New York: Billboard Publications, 1974. $10.95.

An invaluable guide to the business aspects of music that covers copyright, agents, publishing,

labor contracts and agreements, payola, trade
works, taxation, etc. Both volumes include actual
forms and documents.

ANTHOLOGIES AND CHRONOLOGIES

583.   Mattfeld, Julius. <u>Variety Music Cavalcade 1620-
       1969: A Chronology of Vocal and Instrumental
       Music Popular in the United States</u>. 3rd ed.
       Englewood Cliffs, NJ: Prentice-Hall, 1971. $15.00.

       Includes a brief account of the parallel of social
       and historical events occurring each year. With
       a title index.

584.   Slonimsky, Nicolas. <u>Music Since 1900</u>. 4th ed.
       New York: Charles Scribner's Sons, 1971. $49.50.

       The main text is a chronology of important "head-
       lines" of musical events. Contains reproductions
       of contemporary documents, letters, speeches
       which helped shape contemporary music, plus a
       useful dictionary of terms.

MUSIC LITERATURE:
BIOGRAPHIES

    This select list of biographies includes only
those works written in the English language. All of
the titles listed were in print at the time of compilation, at which time (1978) the total price of the
items was $964.45, cloth, and $896.35, paper.
    More extensive biographical listings may be found
in the following pamphlets:

- Public Libraries Commission of the International Association of Music Libraries.
  International Basic List of Literature on
  Music. Den Haag: Nederlands Bibliothek
  en Lectuur Centrum, 1975. $4.50.

- Winesanker, Michael. A List of Books on
  Music. Reston, VN: National Association
  of Schools of Music, 1977. $4.50.

    For other listings of biographies in this compila-
tion, see also AMERICAN MUSIC; Books.

INDIVIDUAL BIOGRAPHIES

BACH (family)
  585. Geiringer, Karl. The Bach Family: Seven
        Generations of Creative Genius. New York:
        Oxford University Press, 1954. $15.00.

BACH, Johann Sebastian, 1685-1750.
  586. David, Hans T. and Arthur Mendel. The Bach
        Reader: A Life in Letters and Documents. Rev.
        ed. New York: W. W. Norton & Co., Inc., 1966.
        Paper, $4.95.

  587. Terry, Charles S. Bach: A Biography. New
        York: Scholarly Press, 1962. $16.00.

BARTÓK, Béla, 1881-1945.
   588.   Stevens, Halsey. <u>The Life and Music of Béla
       Bartók</u>. Rev. ed. New York: Oxford University
       Press, 1964. $12.50.

BEETHOVEN, Ludwig van, 1770-1827.
   589.   Landon, H. C. Robbins. <u>Beethoven: A Documentary
       Study</u>. New York: Macmillan Publishing Co.,
       Inc., 1970. $25.00.

   590.   <u>Thayer's Life of Beethoven</u>. Revised and edited
       by Eliot Forbes. 2v. Princeton, NJ: Princeton
       University Press, 1967. $40.00; paper, $9.95.

BELLINI, Vincenzo, 1801-1835.
   591.   Weinstock, Herbert. <u>Vincenzo Bellini: His Life
       and His Operas</u>. New York: Alfred A. Knopf, Inc.
       $15.00.

BERG, Alban, 1885-1935.
   592.   Carner, Mosco. <u>Alban Berg: The Man & the Work</u>.
       New York: Holmes & Meier Publishers, Inc.,
       1977. $22.00.

BERLIOZ, Hector, 1803-1869.
   593.   Barzun, Jacques. <u>Berlioz and the Romantic
       Century</u>. 3rd ed. New York: Columbia University
       Press, 1969. 2v. $30.00.

BIZET, Georges, 1838-1875.
   594.   Dean, Winton. <u>Bizet</u>. 3rd ed. New York:
       Octagon Books, 1975. $8.50.

BRAHMS, Johannes, 1833-1897.
   595.   Geiringer, Karl. <u>Brahms: His Life and Works</u>.
       2nd ed. London: Allen & Unwin, Ltd., 1948.
       $7.35.

BRITTEN, Benjamin, 1913-   .
   596.   Holst, Imogen. <u>Britten</u>. New York: Thomas Y.
       Crowell Co., 1966. $4.50.

BRUCKNER, Anton, 1824-1896.
   597.   Watson, Derek. <u>Bruckner</u>. The Master Musicians
       Series. Totowa, NJ: Rowan & Littlefield, Inc.,
       1976. $6.50.

BYRD, William, 1542 or 3-1623.
  598. Fellowes, Edmund H. <u>William Byrd</u>. 2nd ed.
      New York: Oxford University Press, 1967. $11.25.

CHAĬKOVSKIĬ, Petr Il'ich, 1840-1893.
  599. Warrack, John. <u>Tchaikovsky</u>. New York: Charles
      Scribner's Sons, Inc., 1973. $12.50.

CHOPIN, Fryderyk Franciszek, 1810-1849.
  600. Walker, Alan, ed. <u>Chopin Companion: Profiles</u>
      <u>of the Man & the Musician</u>. New York: W. W.
      Norton & Co., Inc., 1973. Paper, $4.95.

COPLAND, Aaron, 1900-   .
  601. Dobrin, Arnold. <u>Aaron Copland: His Life and</u>
      <u>Times</u>. New York: Thomas Y. Crowell Co., 1967.
      $4.95.

COUPERIN, François, 1668-1733.
  602. Mellers, Wilfred H. <u>Francois Couperin and the</u>
      <u>French Classical Tradition</u>. New York: Dover
      Publishing Co., Inc., 1972. Paper, $4.50.
      New York: Taplinger Publishing Co., Inc., 1967.
      Cloth, $10.00.

DEBUSSY, Claude, 1862-1918.
  603. Lockspeiser, Edward. <u>Debussy: His Life and</u>
      <u>Mind</u>. New York: Macmillan Publishing Co.,
      Inc., 1962-1965. 2v. $16.00.

DONIZETTI, Gaetano, 1797-1848.
  604. Weinstock, Herbert. <u>Donizetti and the World of</u>
      <u>Opera in Italy, Paris, and Vienna in the First</u>
      <u>Half of the Nineteenth Century</u>. New York:
      Pantheon Books, 1963. $15.00.

DOWLAND, John, 1563-1626.
  605. Poulton, Diana. <u>John Dowland: His Life and</u>
      <u>Works</u>. Berkeley: University of California
      Press, 1972. $30.00.

DVOŘÁK, Antonín, 1841-1904.
  606. Clapham, John. <u>Antonín Dvořák</u>. New York: St.
      Martin's Press, 1966. $20.00.

FAURÉ, Gabriel Urbain, 1845-1924.
  607. Koechlin, Charles L. Gabriel Faure, 1845-1924.
      (Repr. of 1945 ed.). Philadelphia: American
      Musicological Society Press, 1976. $8.50.

FRANCK, César Auguste, 1822-1890.
  608. Davies, Laurence. Cesar Franck and His Circle.
      New York: Da Capo Press, 1977. (Repr. of 1970
      ed.). $19.50.

GABRIELI, Giovanni, 1557-1612.
  609. Arnold, Denis. Giovanni Gabrieli. New York:
      Oxford University Press, 1974. Paper, $6.00.

GERSHWIN, George, 1898-1937.
  610. Schwartz, Charles. Gershwin: His Life and Music.
      London: Abelard-Schuman, Ltd., 1974. $11.00.

GRIEG, Edvard Hagerup, 1843-1907.
  611. Horton, John. Grieg. The Master Musicians
      Series. London: J. M. Dent & Sons, Ltd.,
      1974. $5.50.

HÄNDEL, Georg Friedrich, 1685-1759.
  612. Lang, Paul Henry. George Frederic Handel.
      New York: W. W. Norton & Co., Inc., 1966.
      $20.00.

HAYDN, Joseph, 1732-1809.
  613. Geiringer, Karl. Haydn: a Creative Life in
      Music. 2nd ed. Berkeley: University of
      California Press, 1968. $13.75; paper, $4.50.

HINDEMITH, Paul, 1895-1963.
  614. Skelton, Geoffrey. Paul Hindemith: The Man
      Behind the Music. Atlantic Highlands, NJ:
      Humanities Press Inc., 1975. $15.00.

HOLST, Gustav, 1874-1934.
  615. Holst, Imogen. The Music of Gustav Holst.
      2nd ed. New York: Oxford University Press,
      1968. $5.00.

IVES, Charles Edward, 1874-1954.
> 616.   Hitchcock, H. Wiley. _Ives_. Oxford Studies of
>   Composers. New York: Oxford University Press,
>   1977. Paper, $7.25.

> 617.   Rossiter, Frank. _Charles Ives and His America_.
>   New York: Liveright Publishing Corp., 1975.
> $15.00. See also AMERICAN MUSIC: Books.

KODÁLY, Zoltán, 1882-1967.
> 618.   Eosze, Laszol. _Zoltan Kodaly: His Life and Work_.
>   Boston: Crescendo Publishing Co., 1969. $7.50.

LISZT, Franz, 1811-1886.
> 619.   Walker, Alan. _Liszt_. London: Faber & Faber,
>   Inc., 1971. $2.50.

MAHLER, Gustav, 1860-1911.
> 620.   Blaukopf, Kurt, ed. _Mahler: A Documentary
>   Study_. New York: Oxford University Press,
>   1976. $37.50.

> 621.   La Grange, Henry-Louis de. _Mahler_. Vol. 1.
>   New York: Doubleday & Co., Inc., 1973. $17.50.

MENDELSSOHN-BARTHOLDY, Felix, 1809-1847.
> 622.   Jacob, Heinrich E. _Felix Mendelssohn & His
>   Times_. Westport, CT: Greenwood Press, Inc.,
>   1973. $17.25.

MESSIAEN, Oliver, 1908-   .
> 623.   Johnson, Robert Sherlaw. _Messiaen_. Berkeley:
>   University of California Press, 1975. $18.50.

MILHAUD, Darius, 1892-1974.
> 624.   Milhaud, Darius. _Notes without Music: An Auto-
>   biography_. Translated by Donald Evans. 1953.
>   Reprint. New York: Da Capo Press, Inc., 1970.
> $17.50.

MONTEVERDI, Claudio, 1567-1643.
> 625.   Arnold, Denis. _Monteverdi_. The Master
>   Musicians Series. London: J. M. Dent & Sons,
>   Ltd., 1963. $8.50.

MOZART, Johann Chrysostom Wolfgang Amadeus, 1756-1791.
   626. Deutsch, Otto Erich. Mozart: A Documentary
      Biography. Stanford, CA: University Press,
      1966. $20.00.

   627. Einstein, Alfred. Mozart: His Character, His
      Work. New York: Oxford University Press, 1945.
      $15.00; 1965. Paper, $4.95.

MUSORGSKIĬ, Modest Petrovich, 1839-1881.
   628. Calvocoressi, M. C. Modest Mussorgsky: His
      Life and Works. The Master Musician Series.
      London: J. M. Dent & Sons, Ltd., 1974. $5.00.

PALESTRINA, Giovanni, 1525?-1594.
   629. Roche, Jerome. Palestrina. Oxford Studies of
      Composers Series. New York: Oxford University
      Press, 1971. $4.50.

PROKOF'EV, Sergeĭ Sergeevich, 1891-1953.
   630. Nestyev, Israel. Prokofiev. Stanford, CA:
      University Press, 1960. $17.50.

PUCCINI, Giacomo, 1858-1924.
   631. Carner, Mosco. Puccini: A Critical Biography.
      2nd ed. London: Duckworth, 1975. $24.00.

PURCELL, Henry, 1658 or 9-1695.
   632. Westrup, Jack A. Purcell. The Master Musicians
      Series. New York: Octagon Books, 1975. $8.50.

RACHMANINOFF, Sergei, 1873-1943.
   633. Bertensson, Sergei & Jay Leyda. Sergei Rachma-
      ninoff: A Lifetime in Music. New York: New
      York University Press, 1956. $10.00.

RAMEAU, Jean Philippe, 1683-1764.
   634. Girdlestone, Cuthbert. Jean-Philippe Rameau:
      His Life and Work. Rev. ed. New York: Dover
      Publishing Co., 1970. $7.75.

RAVEL, Maurice, 1875-1937.
   635. Orenstein, Arbie. Ravel: Man and Musician.
      New York: Columbia University Press, 1975.
      $12.50.

RIMSKIĬ-KORSAKOV, Nikolaĭ Andreevich, 1844-1908.
636. Rimskiĭ-Korsakov, Nikolaĭ. <u>My Musical Life</u>.
Translated by Judith A. Joffe. 3rd ed. rev.
New York: Vienna House, Inc., 1972. $18.00.

ROSSINI, Gioacchino Antonio, 1792-1868.
637. Weinstock, Herbert. <u>Rossini: A Biography</u>. New
York: Alfred A. Knopf Inc., 1968. $12.50.

SATIE, Eric, 1866-1925.
638. Harding, James. <u>Erik Satie</u>. London: Seeker
& Warburg, 1975. $12.50.

SCARLATTI, Domenico, 1685-1757.
639. Kirkpatrick, Ralph. <u>Domenico Scarlatti</u>. Rev.
ed. Princeton, NJ: Princeton University Press,
1955. $18.50.

SCHÖNBERG, Arnold, 1874-1951.
640. Stuckenschmidt, H. H. <u>Arnold Schoenberg:
His Life, World, and Work</u>. Translated by
Humphrey Searle. London: John Calder, 1977.
$22.50.

SCHUBERT, Franz Peter, 1797-1828.
641. Deutsch, Otto Erich. <u>Schubert: A Documentary
Biography</u>. 1946. Reprint. Translated by
Eric Blom. New York: Da Capo Press, 1977.
$45.00.

642. Einstein, Alfred. <u>Schubert: A Musical Portrait</u>.
New York: Vienna House, 1976. Paper, $3.95.

SCHUMANN, Robert Alexander, 1810-1856.
643. Walker, Alan, ed. <u>Robert Schumann: The Man and
His Music</u>. New York: Barnes & Noble, 1974.
$15.00.

SIBELIUS, Jean, 1865-1957.
644. Layton, Robert. <u>Sibelius</u>. New York: Octagon
Books, 1966. $8.50.

SKRIABIN, Aleksandr Nikolaevich, 1872-1915.
645. Bowers, Faubion. <u>The New Scriabin: Enigma and
Answers</u>. New York: St. Martin's Press, Inc.,
1973. $8.95; paper, $3.95.

STOCKHAUSEN, Karlheinz, 1928-   .
   646. Wörner, Karl H. Stockhausen: Life and Work.
      London: Faber & Faber, Inc., 1973. $2.50.

STRAUSS, Richard, 1864-1949.
   647. Kennedy, Michael. Richard Strauss. The Master
      Musicians Series. Totowa, NJ: Rowman & Little-
      field, Inc., 1976. $8.50.

STRAVINSKII, Igor' Fedorovich, 1882-1971.
   648. White, Eric W. Stravinsky: The Composer and
      His Works. Berkeley: University of California
      Press, 1966. $18.50.

SULLIVAN, Arthur Seymour, Sir, 1842-1900.
   649. Allen, Reginald. Sir Arthur Sullivan: Composer
      and Personage. New York: Pierpont Morgan
      Library, 1975. $15.00.

TELEMANN, Georg Philipp, 1681-1767.
   650. Petzoldt, Richard. Georg Philipp Telemann.
      New York: Oxford University Press, 1974.
      $7.50.

VARÈSE, Edgard, 1883-1965.
   651. Ouellete, Fernard. Edgard Varese. Translated
      by Derek Coltman. London: Calder & Boyars,
      1973. $6.80; 1975. Paper, $3.35.

VAUGHAN WILLIAMS, Ralph, 1872-1958.
   652. Day, James. Vaughan Williams. 3rd ed. The
      Master Musicians Series. London: J. M. Dent &
      Sons, Ltd., 1975. $6.80; 1973. Paper, $2.00.

VERDI, Giuseppe, 1813-1901.
   653. Weaver, William, ed. Verdi: A Documentary Study.
      London: Thames & Hudson, 1973. $37.50.

   654. Wechsberg, Joseph. Verdi. New York: G. P.
      Putnam's Sons, 1974. $15.00.

VIVALDI, Antonio, 1678-1741.
   655. Kolneder, Walter. Antonio Vivaldi: His Life
      and Work. Berkeley: University of California
      Press, 1970. $16.50.

WAGNER, Richard, 1813-1883.
  656. Barth, Herbert, et al. Wagner: A Documentary
        Study. New York: Oxford University Press,
        1975. $37.50.

  657. Newman, Ernest. Wagner as Man and Artist.
        London: Jonathan Cape, Ltd., 1969. Paper,
        $1.80.

WEBERN, Anton von, 1883-1945.
  658. Kolneder, Walter. Anton Webern: An Introduction
        to His Works. Berkeley: University of California
        Press, 1968. $12.50.

WOLF, Hugo, 1860-1903.
  659. Walker, Frank. Hugo Wolf: A Biography. New
        York: Alfred A. Knopf, Inc., 1968. $15.00.

COMPOSITE BIOGRAPHIES

660. Farga, Franz. Violins and Violinists. Rev. and
      enl. ed. New York: Praeger Publishers, 1969.
      $10.00.

661. Loesser, Arthur. Men, Women, and Pianos. New
      York: Simon & Schuster, Inc., 1974. $9.95.

662. Pleasants, Henry. Great American Popular Singers.
      New York: Simon & Schuster, Inc., 1974. $9.95.

663. _____. Great Singers: From the Dawn of Opera
      to Our Time. New York: Simon & Schuster, Inc., 1966.
      $8.95; paper, $3.95.

664. Schonberg, Harold. Great Conductors. 2nd ed.
      New York: Simon & Schuster, Inc., 1967. $9.95;
      paper, $3.95.

BIOGRAPHIES IN PUBLISHERS' SERIES

665. Abraham, Gerald, ed. BBC Music Guides. Seattle:
      University of Washington. 1969-   .

      Brief analyses of works by major composers (e.g.,
      Bach Cantatas, Beethoven Piano Sonatas, etc.).
      33 volumes to date.

666. Kallin, Anna and Nicholas Nabokov, eds. Twentieth-
      Century Composers. New York: Holt, Rinehart and
      Winston. 1971-   .

      Collective biographies treated according to geo-
      graphical region (e.g., American Music Since
      1910, Germany and Central Europe, etc.) 3 volumes
      to date.

667. Mason, Colin, ed. Oxford Studies of Composers.
      London: Oxford University Press. 1965-   .

      A series of short biographies of composers
      including, for the most part, those who have not
      been treated extensively in the English language,
      especially pre-Baroque and twentieth-century
      composers. 13 volumes to date. Titles from this
      series which were cited in INDIVIDUAL BIOGRAPHIES
      include Ives and Palestrina.

668. Westrup, Jack A., ed. The Master Musicians
      Series. London: J. M. Dent & Sons, Ltd. 1954-   .

      As indicated by the title, this is a biographical
      series which covers major composers of all cen-
      turies. Each volume includes valuable appendices:
      calendar, catalogue of works, personalia, and
      bibliography. 34 volumes to date. Titles from
      this series which were cited in INDIVIDUAL BIO-
      GRAPHIES include Bruckner, Grieg, Monteverdi,
      Mussorgsky, Purcell, Strauss, and Vaughan Williams.

M U S I C   L I T E R A T U R E:
A M E R I C A N   M U S I C: B O O K S

This list covers books about American music including music of the American Indian, folk music, Black
music, jazz, and popular music. It has not been annotated since extensive listings with full annotations
can be found in David Horn's The Literature of American
Music in Books and Folk Music Collections: A Fully
Annotated Bibliography, Metuchen, NJ: Scarecrow Press,
1977. $20.00. This title is highly recommended for
anyone building a collection in American Music. Other
sources for literature on American music include Richard
Jackson's United States Music: Sources of Bibliography
and Collective Biography. Brooklyn: Institute for
Studies in American Music, 1973, Paper, $4.00, and
Gilbert Chase's America's Music (second item below).

Several of the titles in this list are basically
song books but have been included here because they
include descriptions of various types of American song
literature and would be important additions to a small
book collection on American music.

In 1978 the total price of the items, clothbound
preferred, was $1146.00, plus $724.50 for the periodical
Modern Music. For paperback editions preferred the cost
was $1025.00, plus $632.50 for Modern Music. Eight
titles ($175.00, cloth/$168.00, paper) in this list also
appear in the list of reference books; these entries
include the indication "see also REFERENCE BOOKS."

GENERAL WORKS

669. Bio-Bibliographical Index of Musicians in the
      United States of America Since Colonial Times.
      2nd ed. New York: AMS Press, 1971. $20.00.

670. Chase, Gilbert, ed. The American Composer Speaks:
     A Historical Anthology, 1770-1965. Baton Rouge:
     Louisiana State University Press, 1966. $12.50.

671. _____. America's Music: From the Pilgrims to
     the Present. 2nd rev. ed. New York: McGraw-Hill,
     1966. $15.00.

672. Claghorn, Charles Eugene. Biographical Dictionary
     of American Music. Englewood Cliffs, NJ: Prentice-
     Hall, 1973. $12.95.

673. Eagon, Angelo. Catalog of Published Concert
     Music by American Composers. 2nd ed. Metuchen,
     NJ: The Scarecrow Press, 1969. $7.50.

674. _____. Catalog of Published Concert Music by
     American Composers. Supplement to the Second
     Edition. Metuchen, NJ: The Scarecrow Press,
     1971. $6.00.

675. _____. Catalog of Published Concert Music by
     American Composers. Second Supplement to the
     Second Edition. Metuchen, NJ: The Scarecrow
     Press, 1974. $6.00.

676. Hart, Philip. Orpheus in the New World: The
     Symphony Orchestra as an American Cultural
     Institution. New York: W. W. Norton & Co., Inc.,
     1973. $20.00.

677. Hitchcock, H. Wiley. Music in the United States:
     A Historical Introduction. 2nd ed. Englewood
     Cliffs, NJ: Prentice-Hall, 1974. $10.50; paper,
     $6.95.

678. Marrocco, W. Thomas and Harold Gleason. Music
     in America: An Anthology from the Landing of the
     Pilgrims to the Close of the Civil War, 1620-1865.
     New York: W. W. Norton & Co., Inc., 1974. Paper,
     $10.00.

679. Mellers, Wilfrid. Music in a New Found Land: Two
     Hundred Years of American Music. New York:
     Stonehill Publishing Co., 1964. Paper, $5.95.

680. Pavlakis, Christopher. The American Music Hand-
     book. New York: The Free Press, 1974. $25.00.
     See also REFERENCE BOOKS.

681. Stevenson, Robert. Protestant Church Music in
     America . . . from 1564 to the Present: A Short
     Survey of Men and Movements. New York: W. W.
     Norton & Co., Inc., 1970. Paper, $2.95.

EIGHTEENTH-CENTURY MUSIC

682. Lowens, Irving. Music and Musicians in Early
     America. New York: W. W. Norton & Co., Inc.,
     1964. $10.95.

683. McKay, David and Richard Crawford. William
     Billings of Boston: Eighteenth-Century Composer.
     Princeton, NJ: Princeton University Press, 1975.
     $17.50.

684. Pratt, Waldo S. The Music of the Pilgrims. New
     York: Russell & Russell, 1971 (repr. of 1921 ed.).
     $8.00.

685. Sonneck, Oscar G. Early Concert Life in America:
     1731-1800. New York: Adler, 1964 (repr. of
     1907 ed.). $25.00. New York: Dover Publishing
     Co., 1974. Paper, $3.00.

686. _____. Early Opera in America. New York: Arno
     Press, 1963 (repr. of 1915 ed.). $15.00.

NINETEENTH-CENTURY MUSIC

687. Austin, William W. "Susanna," "Jeanie," and "The
     Old Folks at Home": The Songs of Stephan C.
     Foster from His Time to Ours. New York:
     Macmillan, 1975. $17.95.

688. Bierley, Paul E. John Philip Sousa: American
     Phenomenon. Englewood Cliffs, NJ: Prentice-Hall,
     1975. $11.95.

689. _____. John Philip Sousa: A Descriptive Catalog
     of His Works. Music in American Life Series.
     Urbana: University of Illinois Press, 1973. $10.00.

690. Crawford, Richard. The Civil War Songbook: Complete Original Sheet Music for 37 Songs. New York: Dover Publishing Co., 1976. Paper, $5.00.

691. Gilman, Lawrence. Edward MacDowell: A Study. 2nd ed. New York: Da Capo Press, Inc., 1969 (repr. of 1908 ed.). $10.00.

692. Glass, Paul. Singing Soldiers: A History of the Civil War in Song. New York: Da Capo Press, Inc., 1975 (repr. of 1968 ed.). Paper, $4.95.

693. Gottschalk, Louis M. Notes of a Pianist. Edited by Jeanne Behrend. New York: Alfred A. Knopf, Inc., 1974. $7.95.

694. Mussulman, Joseph A. Music in the Cultured Generation: A Social History of Music in America, 1870-1900. Pi Kappa Lambda Studies in American Music. Evanston, IL: Northwestern University Press, 1971. $9.75.

695. Upton, William T. Anthony Philip Heinrich: A Nineteenth Century Composer in America. New York: AMS Press, 1967 (repr. of 1939 ed.). $10.00.

TWENTIETH-CENTURY MUSIC

696. Berger, Arthur. Aaron Copland. Westport, CT: Greenwood, 1971 (repr. of 1953 ed.). $10.75.

697. Cage, John. Silence: Lectures and Writings. Middleton, CT: Wesleyan University Press, 1961. $12.50; paper, $4.25.

698. Copland, Aaron. The New Music: 1900-1960. Rev. ed. New York: W. W. Norton & Co., Inc., 1968. $7.50; paper, $2.45.

699. Cowell, Henry, comp. American Composers on American Music. 2nd ed. New York: Frederick Ungar Publishing Co., 1962. $6.50; paper, $1.95.

700. Cowell, Henry and Sidney Cowell. Charles Ives
and His Music. New York: Oxford University Press,
1969. Paper, $3.50.

701. Edwards, Allen. Flawed Words and Stubborn
Sounds: A Conversation with Elliott Carter.
New York: W. W. Norton & Co., Inc., 1972.
$7.95.

702. Hamm, Charles E., Bruno Nettl, and Ronald
Byrnside. Contemporary Music & Music Cultures.
Englewood Cliffs, NJ: Prentice-Hall, 1975. $9.95.

703. Ives, Charles E. Essays Before a Sonata, the
Majority, and Other Writings. Edited by Howard
Boatwright. New York: W. W. Norton & Co., Inc.,
1970. Paper, $3.25.

704. _____. Memos. Edited by John E. Kirkpatrick.
New York: W. W. Norton & Co., Inc., 1972. $15.00.

705. Kostelanetz, Richard, comp. John Cage. New
York: Praeger Publishers, 1970. Paper, $4.95.

706. Modern Music: A Quarterly Review. 23 v. New
York: AMS Press, Reprint of 1924-1946 ed.
$724.50; paper, $632.50.

707. Perlis, Vivian. Charles Ives Remembered: An Oral
History. 2nd ed. New Haven, CT: Yale University
Press, 1974. $12.50. New York: W. W. Norton &
Co., Inc., 1976. Paper, $3.95.

708. Rossiter, Frank R. Charles Ives and His America.
New York: Liveright Publishing Corp., 1975.
$15.00. See also BIOGRAPHIES.

709. Schwartz, Charles. Gershwin: His Life and Music.
Indianapolis: Bobbs, Merrill Co., Inc., 1973.
$15.00.

710. Thomson, Virgil. American Music Since 1910.
New York: Holt, Rinehart and Winston, 1971.
Paper, $2.95.

711. _____. Virgil Thomson. New York: Alfred A.
Knopf, Inc., 1966. $8.95.

712. Varèse, Louise. Varèse: A Looking Glass Diary.
      New York: W. W. Norton & Co., Inc., 1972.
      $10.00.

AMERICAN INDIAN MUSIC

713. Densmore, Frances. The American Indians and
      Their Music. American Studies. New York:
      Johnson Reprint, 1970 (repr. of 1926 ed.).
      $9.75.

714. Haywood, Charles. A Bibliography of North
      American Folklore and Folksong. Vol. 2.
      The American Indians. 2nd rev. ed. New York:
      Dover Publishing Co., 1961. $15.00. See also
      REFERENCE BOOKS.

715. Nettl, Bruno. North American Indian Musical
      Styles. American Folklore Society Memoir Series,
      No. 45. Austin: University of Texas Press, 1954.
      Paper, $2.95.

FOLK MUSIC

716. Abrahams, Roger D. and George Foss. Anglo-
      American Folksong Style. Englewood Cliffs, NJ:
      Prentice-Hall, 1968. Paper, $4.25.

717. Artis, Bob. Bluegrass. New York: Hawthorne
      Books, Inc. $9.95. New York: Nordon Publications
      Inc. Paper, $1.75.

718. Carawan, Guy and Candy Carawan. Voices from the
      Mountains. New York: Alfred A. Knopf, Inc.,
      1975. Paper, $8.95.

719. Denisoff, R. Serge. Great Day Coming: Folk Music
      and the American Left. Music in American Life
      Series. Urbana: University of Illinois Press,
      1971. $7.50.

720. Haywood, Charles. A Bibliography of North
      American Folklore and Folksong. Vol. 1. The
      American People. 2nd rev. ed. New York: Dover
      Publishing Co., 1961. $15.00. See also
      REFERENCE BOOKS.

721. Lawless, Ray M. Folksingers and Folksongs in America: A Handbook, Biography, Bibliography, and Discography. Rev. ed. New York: Hawthorn Books, Inc., 1965. $12.95.

722. Lomax, Alan. The Folk Songs of North America. Garden City, NY: Doubleday, 1975. $14.95; paper, $6.95.

723. Sandberg, Larry and Dick Weissman. Folk Music Sourcebook. New York: Alfred A. Knopf, Inc. $15.00; paper, $8.95. See also REFERENCE BOOKS.

724. Stambler, Irwin and Grelun Landon. Encyclopedia of Folk, Country and Western Music. New York: St. Martin's Press, 1969. $17.50.

BLACK MUSIC

725. Blesh, Rudi and Harriet Janis. They All Played Ragtime. Rev. ed. New York: Oak Publications, 1971. Paper, $5.95.

726. Courlander, Harold. Negro Folk Music, U.S.A. New York: Columbia University Press, 1963. $15.00; paper, $3.95.

727. Epstein, Dena. Sinful Tunes and Spirituals: Black Folk Music to the Civil War. Music in American Life Series. Urbana: University of Illinois Press, 1977. $17.95.

728. Jones, LeRoi. Blues People: Negro Music in White America. New York: Wm. Morrow & Co., Inc., 1963. $9.95; paper, $2.25.

729. Keil, Charles. Urban Blues. Chicago: University of Chicago Press, 1963. $10.00. Paper, 1966, $2.45.

730. Schafer, William J. and Johannes Riedel. The Art of Ragtime: Form and Meaning of an Original Black American Art. Baton Rouge: Louisiana State University Press, 1973. $10.00.

731. Southern, Eileen. The Music of Black Americans:
A History. New York: W. W. Norton, 1971. $12.50;
paper, $4.95.

732. _____, ed. Readings in Black American Music.
New York: W. W. Norton & Co., Inc., 1972.
$12.50; paper, $4.95.

733. White, Newman I. American Negro Folksongs.
Detroit: Gale Research, 1965 (repr. of 1982 ed.).
$10.00.

JAZZ

734. Coker, Jerry. Improvising Jazz. Englewood
Cliffs, NJ: Prentice-Hall, 1964. Paper, $2.95.

735. Feather, Leonard. The Encyclopedia of Jazz.
New York: Horizon Press, 1960. $17.50. See also
REFERENCE BOOKS.

736. _____. Encyclopedia of Jazz in the Sixties.
New York: Horizon Press, 1967. $17.50. See
also REFERENCE BOOKS.

737. _____ and Ira Gitler. The Encyclopedia of
Jazz in the Seventies. New York: Horizon Press,
1976. $20.00. See also REFERENCE BOOKS.

738. Hentoff, Nat. The Jazz Life. New York: Da Capo
Press. $12.75.

739. Hodeir, André. Jazz: Its Evolution and Essence.
Translated by David Noakes. New York: Da Capo,
1975 (repr. of 1956 ed.). $12.75.

740. Jones, LeRoi. Black Music. New York: Wm.
Morrow & Co., Inc., 1967. Paper, $2.95.

741. Keepnews, Orrin and Bill Grauer. A Pictorial
History of Jazz: People and Places from New
Orleans to Modern Jazz. New ed., revised by
Orrin Keepnews. New York: Crown, 1968. $12.95.

742. Ostransky, Leroy. The Anatomy of Jazz. Westport,
      CT: Greenwood Press, 1973 (repr. of 1960 ed.).
      $18.50.

743. Panassie, Hugues and Madeleine Gautier. Guide to
      Jazz. Translated by Desmond Flower. Westport, CT:
      Greenwood Press, 1973 (repr. of 1956 ed.). $18.50.

744. Schuller, Gunther. Early Jazz: Its Roots and
      Musical Development. New York: Oxford University
      Press, 1968. $13.95.

745. Simon, George. The Big Bands. Rev. ed. New York:
      Macmillan, 1971. $10.00. Paper, rev. enl. ed.,
      1975, $3.95.

746. Tirro, Frank. Jazz: A History. New York: W. W.
      Norton & Co., Inc., 1977. $12.95.

POPULAR CURRENTS

747. Belz, Carl. The Story of Rock. 2nd ed. New
      York: Oxford University Press, 1972. $9.95.

748. Ewen, David. American Popular Songs from the
      Revolutionary War to the Present. New York:
      Random House Inc., 1966. $15.00.

749. _____. Great Men of American Popular Song.
      Rev. enl. ed. Englewood Cliffs, NJ: Prentice-
      Hall, 1972. $14.95.

750. _____. New Complete Book of the American
      Musical Theatre. Rev. ed. New York: Holt, Rine-
      hart and Winston, 1970. $15.00.

751. Gillett, Charles. The Sound of the City: The Rise
      of Rock and Roll. 2nd ed. New York: Dell, 1972.
      Paper, $1.25.

752. Green, Stanley. The World of Musical Comedy.
      Rev. 2nd ed. Cranbury, NJ: A. S. Barnes, 1974.
      $17.50.

753. Lewine, Richard and Alfred Simon. Songs of the
      American Theatre: A Comprehensive Listing of
      More Than 12,000 Songs, Including Selected Titles
      from Film and Television Productions. New York:
      Dodd, Mead & Co., 1973. $15.00. See also
      REFERENCE BOOKS.

754. McCarty, Clifford. Film Composers in America:
      A Checklist of Their Work. New York: Da Capo
      Press, Inc., 1972 (repr. of 1953 ed.). $8.95.

755. Malone, Bill C. Country Music·U.S.A.: A Fifty
      Year History. American Folklore Society Memoirs
      Series, No. 54. Austin: University of Texas
      Press, 1969. $15.00; paper, $4.95.

756. Mattfeld, Julius. Variety Music Cavalcade, 1620-
      1969. 3rd ed. Englewood Cliffs, NJ: Prentice-
      Hall, 1971. $15.00. See also REFERENCE BOOKS.

757. Pleasants, Henry. The Great American Popular
      Singers. New York: Simon & Schuster, 1974.
      $9.95.

758. Shapiro, Nat. Popular Music: An Annotated Index
      of American Popular Songs. 6v. New York: Adrian
      Press, 1964-1973. vols. 1, 2, 4, 5, $16.00;
      vols. 3, 6, $18.50. (v. 1 1950-1959, v. 2 1940-
      1939, v. 3 1960-1964, v. 4 1930-1939, v. 5 1920-
      1929, v. 6 1965-1969.

759. Spaeth, Sigmund. A History of Popular Music in
      America. New York: Random House, 1948. $10.00.

760. Stambler, Irwin. Encyclopedia of Pop, Rock & Soul.
      New York: St. Martin's Press Inc., 1975. $19.95.
      See also REFERENCE BOOKS.

761. Toll, Robert C. Blacking Up: The Minstrel Show
      in Nineteenth-Century America. New York: Oxford
      University Press, 1974. $12.50.

762. Wilder, Alec. American Popular Song: The Great
      Innovators, 1900-1950. Edited and with an Intro-
      duction by James T. Mehler. New York: Oxford
      University Press, 1972. $17.50.

MUSIC LITERATURE:
PERIODICALS AND YEARBOOKS

This basic list of music periodicals and yearbooks is designed as a guide to the most frequently consulted titles in all areas of musical interest. Full ordering information is given, and the annotations offer an indication of the scope, content, and special features of each journal.

Although opinions will always vary, items given a double asterisk (**) may be considered the most basic; asterisked (*) journals are frequently held in medium-size libraries, and the rest of the items indicate titles that will give breadth to any collection of music periodicals. The annual subscription price for the entire list in 1978 was $600.00; the sixteen asterisked (*) titles cost $149.25; and the five double asterisked (**) journals total $77.00.

The primary indexing and abstracting sources for periodical literature in music are Music Index and the International Repertory of Music Literature, RILM Abstracts of Musical Literature. These sources are described in the list, REFERENCE BOOKS.

763. ASCAP Today. New York: American Society of Composers, Authors, and Publishers, v. 1, 1967- .
Free.

Society news published by its public relations committee. Three issues annually.

764. American Choral Review. New York: American Choral Foundation, v. 1, 1958- . $20.00.

A quarterly publication of the Association of Choral Conductors containing some analytical articles on important compositions. Includes book reviews, choral news, lists of new publications.

765. <u>American Music Teacher</u>. Cincinnati: Music Teachers
      National Association. v. 1, 1951-   . $4.00.

      For both private teachers and school teachers,
      this bimonthly journal contains articles, reviews,
      announcement of meetings, contests, etc.

766. *American Musicological Society. <u>Journal</u>. Phila-
      delphia: American Musicological Society, v. 1,
      1948-   . $15.00.

      Published three times a year, JAMS provides
      articles and reviews of a scholarly nature,
      filling the need for a purely musicological
      periodical in the United States.

767. <u>American Recorder</u>. New York: American Recorder
      Society, v. 1, 1959-   . $5.00.

      Includes articles on music and performance for the
      recorder, reviews of music reference tools,
      advertisements of music and wind instruments.
      Quarterly.

768. <u>BMI: The Many Worlds of Music</u>. New York: Broad-
      cast Music, Inc., v. 1, 1962-   . Free.

      Society news for Broadcast Music, Inc. Published
      irregularly.

769. <u>Billboard</u>. Los Angeles: Billboard Publications,
      Inc., v. 1, 1894-   . $50.00.

      For the music-record-tape industries. Includes
      charts for all recording categories, record reviews,
      news reports, statistical studies for the manu-
      facturing, distributing, programming, and re-
      tailing segments of the industry. Weekly.

770. *<u>The Black Perspective in Music</u>. Cambria Heights,
      NY: Foundation for Research in Afro-American
      Creative Arts, v. 1, 1973-   . $5.00.

      The semiannual journal includes well documented
      articles with valuable bibliographies. "In
      Retrospect" highlights the contributions of black

performers from the past. Other departments
cover new books, dissertations, recent recordings,
book reviews, and obituaries.

771. *Clavier: A Magazine for Pianists and Organists.
      Evanston, IL: Instrumentalist Co., v. 1, 1962-   .
      $7.00.

      This bimonthly periodical is the learned journal
      for keyboard teachers and performers. Includes
      analytical and critical articles on keyboard works,
      performance, and instruction. New books, piano
      and organ compositions, and recordings are
      reviewed.

772. Contemporary Keyboard: The Magazine for All Key-
      board Players. Saratoga, CA: GPI Publications,
      v. 1, 1975-   . $12.00.

      As the title indicates, the magazine covers all
      keyboard instruments from harpsichord to syn-
      thesizer and all styles of performance: jazz,
      popular, classical, contemporary. Includes
      record and equipment reviews, numerous articles
      about keyboard performers.

773. Current Musicology. New York: Columbia University
      Department of Music, v. 1, 1965-   . $8.50.

      A semiannual journal devoted to the current state
      of research in musicology. Includes articles,
      bibliographies, criticisms, announcements.

774. The Diapason. Chicago: Diapason, Inc., v. 1,
      1909-   . $7.50.

      A monthly journal devoted to the organ, the harpsi-
      chord, and church music. Includes descriptions
      of new instruments and activities of organists.

775. *Down Beat. Chicago: Maher Publications, v. 1,
      1934-   . $10.00.

      The principal jazz magazine. Published twenty
      times per year, it includes articles and reviews
      of books and records.

776. Early Music. London: Oxford University Press,
      v. 1, 1973-   . $5.80 (£ 3).

      For anyone interested in preclassical music, this
      quarterly journal provides features on instru-
      ments and activities; book, music, and record
      reviews; a music supplement, and an international
      register of players and instrument makers.

777. *Ethnomusicology. New York: Society for Ethno-
      musicology, v. 1, 1958-   . $15.00.

      Containing feature articles and many bibliographies
      and discographies, this title is the most impor-
      tant journal of research in the study of folk
      music, primitive music, and non-Western music.
      Three issues per year.

778. Galpin Society Journal. London: Galpin Society,
      v. 1, 1948-   . $7.75.

      An annual publication of research on musical
      instruments with international coverage. In-
      cludes reviews of music and books.

779. Guitar Player. Los Gatos, CA: Guitar Player
      Publications, v. 1, 1965-   . $8.00.

      Devoted to all areas and styles of guitar playing,
      with much of interest to the folk guitarist,
      including tablatures and instructional articles.
      Monthly.

780. **High Fidelity/Musical America. New York: ABC
      Leisure Magazines, v. 1, 1965-   . $26.00.

      Useful information on performers, the recording
      industry, and the science of sound reproduction
      is found in the High Fidelity section, as well as
      reviews of equipment and popular and classical
      recordings. Musical America provides a chronical
      of musical events and the musicians involved in
      them.

781. *Institute for Studies in American Music. <u>News-</u>
      <u>letter</u>. New York: Brooklyn College Department of
      Music, v. 1, 1971-   . Free.

      Issued semiannually, the <u>Newsletter</u> is a fine
      source of information on current research in
      American music, new books and recordings, acti-
      vities of people and organizations in the field.

782. *<u>Instrumentalist</u>. Evanston, IL: Instrumentalist
      Co., v. 1, 1946-   . $8.00.

      For school and college band and orchestra directors,
      teacher-training specialists in instrumental music
      education, and instrumental teachers.

783. International Folk Music Council. <u>Yearbook</u>.
      Kingston, Ontario: Queen's University Department
      of Music, v. 1, 1949-   . $10.00.

      This <u>Yearbook</u> contains reviews of books, pamphlets
      and recordings of folk music, and the Council's
      proceedings and papers. Articles have an inter-
      national scope. 1949-1968 known as the <u>Journal</u>;
      title changed to <u>Yearbook</u> in 1969.

784. <u>Journal of Band Research</u>. Ames, IA: Iowa State
      University Press, v. 1, 1965-   . $5.00.

      A semiannual publication of the American Band-
      masters Association which includes articles on
      band history and performance, analyses of compo-
      sitions for band, and association news.

785. <u>Journal of Church Music</u>. Philadelphia: Fortress
      Press, v. 1, 1959-   . $7.00.

      In its eleven yearly issues there are articles of
      historical, practical, and general interest. Also
      included are reviews of organ music and commentary
      on anthems. Published by the Lutheran Church of
      America.

786. <u>Journal of Country Music</u>. Nashville, TN: Country
      Music Foundation Press, v. 1, 1970-   . $10.00.

A journal devoted to the publication of articles
treating subjects related to the country music
tradition including country music, old timey music,
bluegrass, western swing, fiddle music, gospel
music, Anglo-American folksong, music research
methodology, recording studio operation, and the
business of music. Three issues per year.

787.   Journal of Jazz Studies. New Brunswick, NJ:
       Rutgers University Institute of Jazz Studies,
       v. 1, 1974-   . $8.00.

       The semiannual journal contains research articles
       with bibliographies and discographies on all
       aspects of jazz.

788.   *Journal of Music Theory. New Haven, CT: Yale
       University, School of Music, v. 1, 1957-   .
       $6.00.

       The semiannual publication contains research
       papers on contemporary and historical theoretical
       problems, extensive bibliographies, and book
       reviews.

789.   Journal of Music Therapy. Lawrence, KA: National
       Association for Music Therapy, v. 1, 1952-   .
       $7.00.

       The quarterly journal publishes papers on training,
       practices, and ideals of the profession.

790.   *Journal of Research in Music Education. Reston,
       VA: Music Educator's National Conference, v. 1,
       1952-   . $8.00.

       This quarterly periodical is the primary source of
       scholarly articles on music education in the
       United States. Research bibliographies, thoroughly
       documented articles, and extensive book reviews
       are its important contributions.

791.   *Music and Letters. London: Music and Letters,
       Ltd., v. 1, 1920-   . $5.80 (£ 3).

International in coverage and published quarterly,
Music and Letters contains articles on music history and style, musicians, critical essays on
recent books, and reviews of music.

792.   **Music Educator's Journal. Reston, VA: Music
        Educator's National Conference, v. 1, 1914-   .
        $8.00.

        A practical journal published nine times per year,
        it contains papers on instruction, concert reviews,
        announcements of contests and awards, activities
        of schools of music, lists of teaching material.

793.   *Music Journal. New York: Music Journal, Inc.,
        v. 1, 1943-   . $11.00.

        Its articles reflect current thought on musical
        topics. Also includes reviews of new books,
        music and records, and musical calendar information.

794.   Music Journal Annual; Anthology. New York: Music
        Journal, Inc., v. 1, 1957-   . $5.00.

        Originally included summary articles and lists of
        music reflecting the year's activities in various
        musical events and publishing. Since 1974 the
        only directory of information included has been on
        schools of music.

795.   **Music Library Association. Notes: The Quarterly
        Journal of the Music Library Association. Ann
        Arbor, MI: Music Library Association, first
        series, 1934-1942; second series, 1943-   .
        $18.00.

        A valuable journal for librarians and music re-
        searchers in all areas, it includes articles,
        bibliographies, and extensive reviews. Regular
        features include Book Reviews, New Reference Books,
        Index to Record Reviews, Music Reviews, Popular
        Music, and Music Received.

796.   *Music Review. Cambridge, England: W. Heffer and
        Sons, Ltd., v. 1, 1940-   . $17.00 (₤ 9).

Comparable to America's Musical Quarterly, this quarterly journal provides papers on musicological subjects, commentary on new works and performers, and critiques of books, scores, and records.

797. Musical America: International Directory of the Performing Arts. Great Barrington, MA: ABC Leisure Magazines, v. 1, 1968-   . $10.00.

An annual supplement to High Fidelity/Musical America, this publication contains directory information.

798. *Musical Quarterly. New York: G. Schirmer, Inc., v. 1, 1915-   . $9.00.

Best known scholarly music periodical in the United States. It includes a quarterly book list and the "Current Chronicle" of concert reviews emphasizes first performances.

799. *Musical Times. London: Novello, v. 1, 1844-   . $10.45.

A monthly publication of the current-events type, it contains articles on music and musicians, concert criticism, reviews. A musical supplement is included with each issue.

800. National Association of Teachers of Singing. Bulletin. Chicago: National Association of Teachers of Singing, Inc., v. 1, 1944-   . $6.00.

Articles cover song style, interpretation and pedagogy; music, books, and records are reviewed in this quarterly.

801. National Music Council. Bulletin. New York: National Music Council, v. 1, 1940-   . $3.50.

This semiannual periodical consists mainly of reports of the activities of the Council and its member organization, thus giving an overview of American musical life.

802. 19th-Century Music. Berkeley: University of
California Press, v. 1, 1977- . $15.00.

The quarterly journal offers scholarly articles,
a section on performers and instruments, book
reviews, and departments for editorial "Viewpoint,
Comment, and Chronicle."

803. **Opera News. New York: Metropolitan Opera Guild,
v. 1, 1865- . $20.00.

Weekly issues relate to the Saturday opera broad-
casts with plot summary, historical notes, and
photographs. Monthly issues cover the national
and international opera scene and history.

804. Perspectives of New Music. Princeton, NJ:
Princeton University Press, v. 1, 1962- .
$9.00.

Published semiannually for the Fromm Music Foundation, the journal contains articles on many
aspects of modern music by composers, critics,
and scholars. Some papers are highly specialized.

805. Pickin'. Philadelphia: North American Publishing
Co., v. 1, 1974- . $12.00.

This monthly periodical includes articles on bluegrass and old-time music, personalities, performance schedules, instruments and repairs,
tablatures, and critical record reviews.

806. Popular Music and Society. Bowling Green, OH:
Bowling Green University, v. 1, 1972- . $6.00.

Contains reviews and articles on popular music,
both current and from earlier decades. Some are
scholarly, others provide lighter reading.

807. Records and Recordings. London: Hansom, v. 1,
1952- . $14.90.

A good source for information on British records
and recording artists containing news of the record
industry and reviews of all kinds of records.

808.   *Rolling Stone. San Francisco, CA: Straight
       Arrow Publishers, v. 1, 1967-   . $14.00.

       A biweekly publication reflecting events and
       trends of the rock music industry. Recordings
       and performers are reviewed.

809.   Sing Out! New York: Sing Out!, Inc., v. 1,
       1950-   . $5.00.

       Covers traditional music of North America,
       particularly the urban movement, with articles
       on various subjects and personalities, instruction,
       tablatures, book and record reviews, and songs.
       Published bimonthly.

810.   *Stereo Review. New York: Ziff-Davis, v. 1,
       1958-   . $8.00.

       Stereo Review, published monthly, consists of
       three sections: "The Equipment," with articles
       on technical data and equipment; "The Music,"
       with reviews of classical and popular records and
       tapes as well as articles on performers; and "The
       Regulars," with editorial comment.

811.   **Tempo: A Quarterly Review of Modern Music.
       London: Boosey & Hawkes, v. 1, 1939-   . $5.00.

       Articles concern contemporary music with some de-
       tailed analysis of new works. Critical reviews
       appear for first performances.

812.   Woodwind World - Brass and Percussion. Oneonta,
       NY: Swift-Dorr, v. 13, 1974-   . $4.00.

       For the professional and the student, this journal
       contains both articles and reviews. It was formed
       by 1975 merger of Woodwind World and Brass &
       Percussion.

813.   World of Music. Mainz: B. Schott's Sohne, v. 1,
       1959-   . $6.70.

       A quarterly journal of the International Music
       Council (UNESCO) in association with the Inter-

national Institute for Comparative Music Studies
and Documentation, Berlin. Articles in English,
French, and German give an overview of the World's
musical activity.

METHODS: INSTRUMENTAL
METHODS AND STUDIES

This select list of instrumental methods and
studies includes method books for each instrument nor-
mally found in a band or orchestra, plus autoharp,
mountain and hammered dulcimer, recorder, harmonica,
guitar, banjo, piano, and organ. Also included are
books for group instruction in strings, brass, orchestra, and band. The annotations are intended to
help in the selection process by giving information
on unique features and instructional approaches. In
1978 the total cost of materials listed was approxi-
mately $1233.00.

STRINGS

Violin

814. Applebaum, Samuel. The Belwin String Builder
     (Violin). Belwin-Mills, 1960. Books One, Two,
     Three: Teacher's manual for each book, $4.00;
     piano accompaniment for each book, $2.50; part
     for each book, $1.75.

     "The Belwin String Builder is a string class
     Method in which the Violin, Viola, Cello, and
     Bass play together throughout. Each book, however,
     is a complete unit and may be used separately for
     class or individual instruction."

815. Dont, Jacob. Etudes and Caprices for Violin,
     Op. 35. Carl Fischer, 1903. $1.50.

816. Kreutzer, Rodolphe. Forty-Two Studies for Violin.
     Edited by Emil Kross. Carl Fischer, 1915. $3.50.

117

817. Suzuki, Shinichi. Suzuki Violin School. Evans-
      ton, IL: Summy-Birchard Co., 1972. v. 1 & 2:
      Vln.-$3.95, Pno.-$4.95, 12" LP-$8.95; v. 3 & 4:
      Vln.-$3.95, Pno.-$5.95, 12" LP-$8.95; v. 5: Vln.-
      $4.95, Pno.-$4.95, 12" LP-$8.95; v. 6: Vln.-
      $4.95, 12" LP-$8.95; v. 7: Vln.-$4.95, Pno.-
      $4.95, 12" LP-$8.95; v. 8: Vln.-$4.95, Pno.-
      $4.95, 12" LP-$8.95; v. 9: Vln.-$4.95, Pno.-
      $4.95; v. 10-$4.95, Pno.-$4.95.

      "Children learn to make music as they learn their
      mother tongue: through hearing it spoken, imi-
      tating the sounds, and gradually attaching meaning
      to them. . . Learning is based on listening."
      (Applies also to piano series.)

818. Wohlfahrt, Franz. Sixty Etudes for Violin, Op.
      45. Revised and fingered by Fred J. Sharp.
      Carl Fischer. 2 books, $1.00 each.

Viola

819. Applebaum, Samuel. The Belwin String Builder
      (Viola). Belwin-Mills, 1960. Books One, Two,
      Three: Teacher's manual for each book, $4.00;
      Piano accompaniment for each book, $2.50; Part
      for each book, $1.75.

820. Kayser, Heinrich Ernest. 36 Studies (Elementary
      and Progressive) for Viola Solo, Op. 20. Trans-
      cribed and edited by Joseph Vieland. Inter-
      national, 1956. $3.00.

821. Kreutzer, Rodolphe. 42 Studies for Viola Solo.
      Edited by Louis Pagels. International. $4.00.

822. Mazas, Jacques Féréol. (30) Etudes Spéciales for
      Viola Solo, Op. 36, Book I. Transcribed by Louis
      Pagels. International. $3.50.

823. _____. (26) Etudes Brillantes for Viola Solo,
      Op. 36, Book II. Transcribed by Louis Pagels.
      International. $3.50.

Violoncello

824.   Applebaum, Samuel. The Belwin String Builder
       (Cello). Belwin-Mills, 1960. Books One, Two,
       Three: Teacher's manual for each book, $4.00;
       Piano accompaniment for each book, $2.50; Part
       for each book, $1.75.

825.   Dotzauer, Justus. 62 Select Studies for Violon-
       cello. Arranged in Progressive Order by Johann
       Klingenberg. Edited by F. Girard. Carl Fischer,
       1914. 2 books, $1.50 each.

826.   Duport, Jean Louis. Twenty-One Etudes for the
       Violoncello. Edited and fingered by Leo Schulz.
       G. Schirmer, 1930. 2 books, $2.00 each.

       Book I contains a biographical sketch of the
       composer by Richard Aldrich.

827.   Klengel, Julius. Technical Studies for the
       Violoncello. G. Schirmer, v. 1. $2.00.

       Uses scales, triads, and broken thirds through
       all the keys in a systematic way.

828.   Lee, Sebastian. Forty Melodic and Progressive
       Etudes for Violoncello, Op. 31. Edited and
       fingered by Leo Schulz. G. Schirmer, 1931.
       Book I, $2.00; Book II, $2.25.

829.   Suzuki, Shinichi. Sato Cello School. Summy-
       Birchard, 1969. v. 1: Cello-$3.95, Pno.-$2.95;
       v. 2: Cello-$3.95, Pno.-$2.95; v. 3: Cello-
       $1.95, Pno.-$2.95; v. 4: Cello-$1.95, Pno.-$2.95;
       v. 5: Cello-$4.95, Pno.-$4.95.

       In English and Japanese.

Double Bass

830.   Applebaum, Samuel. The Belwin String Builder
       (Bass). Belwin-Mills, 1960. Books One, Two,
       Three: Teacher's manual for each book, $4.00;
       Piano accompaniment for each book, $2.50; Part
       for each book, $1.75.

831. Simandl, Franz. New Method for the Double Bass.
      English and German texts. Revised and enlarged
      by F. Zimmerman. Carl Fischer, 1948. 2 books,
      $3.50 each.

      Book I is designed for orchestral playing and
      Book II offers a systematic guide for solo
      playing.

832. _____. Thirty Etudes. Carl Fischer, 1940.
      $2.00.

      "For the acquisition of correct and broad in-
      tonation together with rhythmic precision."

Guitar

833. Montgomery, Wes. Jazz Guitar Method. Text by
      Lee Garson. Music edited by Jimmy Stewart.
      Photography by Charles Stewart. Robbins Music
      Corporation. (Big 3 Music Corporation), 1968.
      $5.95.

834. Noad, Frederick M. Solo Guitar Playing. Collier
      Books (Macmillan), 1968. $3.95.

      Contains graded duet exercises, practice studies,
      a survey of the guitar repertoire, with selections
      and a glossary of musical terms.

835. Sor, Ferdinand. Method for the Spanish Guitar.
      Translated by A. Merrick. New York: Da Capo,
      1971. $12.50.

836. Taussig, Harry. Instrumental Techniques of
      American Folk Guitar. Oak Publications (Music
      Sales Corporation), 1968. $3.95.

      Concerns the use of the guitar in the "traditional"
      manner for instrumental solos and instrumental
      breaks based on the styles of the Carter Family,
      Etta Baker, Elizabeth Cotton, Mississippi John
      Hurt, Chet Atkins, Merle Travis, and others.
      Includes standard notation, tablature, chord
      diagrams, a discography, and a bibliography.

837.   _____. <u>Teach Yourself Guitar</u>. Oak Publications
        (Music Sales Corporation), 1971. $4.95.

838.   Traum, Happy. <u>Flat-Pick Country Guitar</u>. Oak
        Publications (Music Sales Corporation), 1973.
        $3.95.

        Step-by-step instruction from simple patterns
        through the more complicated styles of noted folk
        and blues guitarists, standard music notation
        plus tablature.

Banjo

839.   Rosenbaum, Art. <u>Old-time Mountain Banjo</u>. Oak
        Publications (Music Sales Corporation), 1968.
        $4.95.

        Includes a selected discography.

840.   Seeger, Peter. <u>How to Play the 5-String Banjo</u>:
        <u>A Manual for Beginners</u>. 3rd edition. Oak
        Publications (Music Sales Corporation), 1962.
        $2.95.

        The basic manual for banjo players, with melody
        line, lyrics, and banjo accompaniment and solos
        notated in standard form and tablature.

Autoharp

841.   Peterson, Meg. <u>The Many Ways to Play the Autoharp</u>.
        Oscar Schmidt, 1966. v. 1 & v. 2: $1.50 each;
        $3.00 total.

        Volume 1 is particularly good for those who have
        not played other instruments. Volume 2 is an
        introduction to melody playing and uses a number
        system so that music reading is not essential.

842.   Taussig. Harry. <u>Folk Style Autoharp</u>. Oak
        Publications, 1973. Paper, $3.95.

        A well organized method which is especially good
        for those with some familiarity with the guitar or
        banjo. Includes a history of the autoharp by
        A. Doyle Moore.

Dulcimer and Hammered Dulcimer

843. French, Dorothy and Lynn McSpadden. <u>Brethren We
      Have Met: Traditional Hymns and Carols for the
      Dulcimer</u>. The Dulcimer Shoppe, 1970. $4.95.

      Includes 30 songs with fret numbers and music as
      well as instructions on playing styles, modes,
      and chords.

844. Hellman, Neal and Sally Holden. <u>Life is Like a
      Mountain Dulcimer</u>. TRO, 1974. $3.50.

      33 songs are written in tablature for fingering
      melody, drone, and bass strings. It also in-
      cludes descriptions of right-hand techniques,
      chords, embellishments.

845. Mitchell, Howard W. <u>The Hammered Dulcimer</u>. Folk-
      Legacy Records, 1971. $6.98. Book only, paper,
      $3.50.

      The booklet is enclosed in the record of the same
      name (Folk-Legacy FSI 43), but is available
      separately as well. It gives instruction in
      building the instrument and in five styles of
      playing.

846. _____. <u>The Mountain Dulcimer: How to Make It
      and Play It</u>. Folk-Legacy Records, 1965. $6.98.
      Book only, paper, $3.50.

      Book and record (FSI 29) available separately.
      Discussion of the four-string dulcimer includes
      information on tunings, modes, chord playing, and
      construction. Other dulcimers are discussed.
      For the more advanced player.

847. Ritchie, Jean. <u>The Dulcimer Book</u>. Oak Publi-
      cations, 1964. Paper, $2.95.

      Includes 16 songs written in music and with fret
      numbers. A companion record of the same title from
      Oak Publication includes spoken tuning instructions
      and song examples played by different artists. A
      practical instruction combination.

WOODWINDS

  Flute

848. Andersen, Joachim. Twenty-Four Etudes for the
      Flute in All the Major and Minor Keys, Op. 15.
      New York: Carl Fischer, 1940. $2.50.

849. Cavally, Robert, composer. Melodious and Pro-
      gressive Studies for Flute. San Antonio, TX:
      Southern Music Company, 1958-1969. Books 1 & 2,
      $3.00 each; Book 3, $2.75.

      Studies arranged and revised from Andersen,
      Garibaldi, Koehler, Terschak, Boehm, Kronke,
      and Mollerup.

850. Jacobs, Frederick, William Eisenhauer, and
      Charles F. Gouse. Learn to Play the Flute!
      Alfred Publishing Co., 1969. 2 books, $2.50
      each.

      "A carefully graded method that emphasizes good
      tone production, builds a sound rhythmic sense,
      and develops well-rounded musicianship."
      (Applies to entire series.)

851. Pease, Donald J. Pro Art Flute and Piccolo
      Method. Pro Art. 2 books, $2.00 each.

      "For individual or class instruction." (Applies
      to entire series.)

852. Voxman, Himie. Selected Studies for Flute:
      Advanced Etudes, Scales, and Arpeggios in All
      Major and Minor Keys. Rubank, 1948. $3.00.

853. _____ and William Gower. Rubank Advanced Method,
      Flute. Rubank, 1940-1954. V. 1, $2.50; v. 2,
      $3.00.

      "An outlined course of study designed to follow up
      any of the various elementary and intermediate
      methods." (Applies to entire series.)

Oboe

854.   Andraud, Albert J. Practical and Progressive
       Oboe Method, Reed Making, Melodious and Technical
       Exercises. Text translated by Helen H. Andraud.
       Southern Music Co. $9.00.

       Includes a brief history of the oboe family.

855.   Gekeler, Kenneth. Belwin Oboe Method. Edited
       by Nilo W. Hovey. Belwin-Mills, 1952. 3 books,
       $1.75 each.

856.   MacBeth, James. Learn to Play the Oboe! Alfred
       Publishing Co., 1970. 2 books, $2.50.

857.   Tustin, Whitney. Technical Studies for Treble
       Woodwind Instruments. Peer, 1955. $3.00.

       For flute (and piccolo), oboe (and English horn),
       clarinet (and E flat clarinet, alto clarinet,
       bass clarinet) and saxophone (soprano, alto,
       tenor, baritone, bass). Intermediate and
       advanced players.

858.   Voxman, Himie. Selected Studies for Oboe: Advanced
       Etudes, Scales, and Arpeggios in all Major and
       Minor Keys. Rubank, 1942. $3.00.

859.   _____ and William Gower. Rubank Advanced
       Method, Oboe. Rubank, 1940. V. 1, $2.50.

Clarinet

860.   Baermenn, Karl. Complete Celebrated Method for
       Clarinet, Op. 63. Revised for the Albert and
       Boehm system by Gustave Langenus. Carl Fischer,
       1917. $7.50.

861.   Benham, Charles. Pro Art Clarinet Method. Pro
       Art, 1957. 2 books, $2.00 each.

862.   Hendrickson, Clarence V. Hendrickson Method for
       Clarinet. Belwin-Mills, 1942. Book II, $2.00.

863. Jacobs, Frederick, William Eisenhauer and
     Charles F. Gouse. Learn to Play the Clarinet!
     Alfred Publishing Co., 1969. 2 books, $2.50;
     v. 2, $3.00.

864. Voxman, Himie and William Gower. Rubank Ad-
     vanced Method, Clarinet. Rubank, 1939-1953.
     V. 1, $2.50; v. 2, $3.00.

Alto, Bass, and Contrabass Clarinet

865. Baerman for the Alto and Bass Clarinet. Edited
     by William E. Rhoads. Southern Music Company,
     1963. $3.00.

     "Adapted from Division Three-Celebrated Method
     for Clarinet, Opus 63 by Carl Baermann."

866. Porter, Neal and Fred Weber. Alto Clarinet
     Student: A Method for Individual Instruction.
     Belwin-Mills, 1969. 3 books, $2.00 each.

     Three levels: Elementary, Intermediate, Advanced
     Intermediate. Instructions are highlighted
     with red print. (Applies to entire series.)

867. Rhoads, William E. Bass Clarinet Student: A Method
     for Individual Instruction. Belwin-Mills, 1969.
     3 books, $2.00 each.

868. _____. 18 Selected Studies for Alto and Bass
     Clarinet. Southern Music Company. $1.75.

     The material was taken from the works of
     H. Lazarus, C. Rose, Demnitz Rode, C. Baermann,
     R. Kietzer, Marzas, F. Muller, and Capelle.

869. _____. 35 Technical Studies for Alto and Bass
     Clarinet. Southern Music Company, 1962., $1.75.

870. _____. 21 Foundation Studies for Alto and Bass
     Clarinet Selected from Literature for the Violon-
     cello. Southern Music Company, 1965. $2.25.

     Composers include S. Lee, Dotzauer, Buchler, Piatti,
     C. Schroder, Cossman, Kummer, Merck, and others.

871. Voxman, Himie. <u>Introducing the Alto or Bass
      Clarinet: A Transfer Method for Intermediate
      Instruction</u>. Rubank, 1952. $2.00.

Bassoon

872. Gekeler, Kenneth. <u>Belwin Bassoon Method</u>. Edited
      by Nilo W. Hovey. Belwin-Mills, 1952. 3 books,
      $1.75 each.

873. McDowell, Paul D. <u>Practical Studies for Bassoon</u>.
      Edited by Nilo W. Hovey. Belwin-Mills, 1959-
      1960. 2 books, $2.00 each.

      Intended to supplement any of the elementary
      methods available. Section 1 of each book con-
      tains studies for rhythmic development; section
      2 has scale and technical exercises.

874. Milde, Ludwig. <u>25 Studies in Scales and Chords
      for Bassoon</u>, Opus 25. Edited by Simon Kovar.
      International, 1950. $2.50.

875. Voxman, Himie and William Gower. <u>Rubank Advanced
      Method, Bassoon</u>. Rubank, 1942. V. 1, $2.50.

876. Weissenborn, Julius. <u>Bassoon Studies</u>, Op. 8.
      Carl Fischer, 1940-1941. 2 v., $2.50.

Saxophone

877. Jacobs, Frederick, William Eisenhauer, and
      Charles F. Gouse. <u>Learn to Play the Saxophone</u>!
      Alfred Publishing Co., 1969. 2 books, $2.50
      each.

878. Labanchi, Gaetano. <u>Thirty-Three Concert Etudes</u>.
      Transcribed for saxophone by Gerardo Lasilli.
      Carl Fischer, 1934-1938. 3 v., $2.00 each.

879. Mayeur, L. <u>Grand Collection of Scales, Arpeggio
      Exercises and Studies in Interpretation for
      Saxophone</u>. Edited by W. F. Ambrosio. Carl
      Fischer, 1925. $3.50.

880. Pease, Donald J. Pro Art Saxophone Method.
      Pro Art, 1960-1963. 2 books, $2.00 each.

881. Voxman, Himie and William Gower. Rubank Advanced
      Method, Saxophone. Rubank, 1940-1957. V. 1,
      $2.50; v. 2, $3.00.

Recorder

882. Bradford, Margaret and Elizabeth Parker. How to
      Play the Recorder. G. Schirmer. Soprano
      recorder, 2 books, $1.50 each. Alto recorder,
      2 books, $1.50 each.

      Selected tunes arranged for soprano and alto
      recorders.

883. Nitka, Arthur and Johanna Kulbach. The Recorder
      Guide. Oak Publications, 1955. $14.95. Book
      only, paper, $5.95.

      Soprano and alto recorders taught with the folk
      melodies of many cultures. Includes a record
      which offers separate instruction for soprano
      and also recorder and duets.

884. Tobey, Cliff. A Guide to Playing the Recorder.
      Oak Publications (AMSCO), 1970. $5.95.

      For the beginning player, this is a simple and
      well-organized method. It does not require
      previous experience in reading music.

Harmonica

885. Arnold, Ken. Amazing Grace and Other Gospel
      Sounds for Harmonica. Edward Marks, 1972. $2.00.

      An easy to follow book of 30 songs with words and
      music, chord symbols, and hole numbers. For
      chromatic and marine band harmonicas.

886. Morgan, Tommy. Blues Harmonica. Gwyn Publishing,
      1971. $3.00.

Many musical examples are given with music, chord
symbols, and hole numbers. A cassette is available
from the publisher. For marine band harmonicas
only.

BRASSES

French Horn

887. Alphonse, Maxime. 200 New Studies. LeDuc. Set
      1, $6.25; Sets 2-3, 5-6, $6.45 each; Set 4, $5.65.

888. Getchell, Robert W. Practical Studies for French
      Horn. Belwin-Mills, 1961. 2 books, $2.00 each.

      "Designed to develop chord consciousness, to
      provide experience in the fundamental rhythms,
      key signatures, articulations and to improve
      accuracy in reading." (Applies to entire series.)

889. Gouse, Charles F. and William Eisenhauer. Learn
      to Play the French Horn! Alfred Publishing Co.,
      1970. 2 books, $2.50 each.

890. Gower, William and Himie Voxman. Rubank Advanced
      Method, French Horn. Rubank, 1947-1957. V. 1,
      $2.50; v. 2, $3.00.

891. Petrie, Charles and Donald J. Pease. Pro Art
      French Horn Method in F and E flat. Pro art,
      1960-1964. 2 books, $2.00.

892. Pottag, Max P., editor. Preparatory Melodies to
      Solo Work for French Horn. Belwin-Mills, 1941.
      $2.00.

      "Selected from the famous SCHANTL Collection."

Trumpet - Cornet

893. Arban, Joseph-Jean. Arban's Conservatory Method
      for Trumpet (Trumpet). Revised abridged edition
      edited by Edwin Franko Goldman and William M.
      Smith. Carl Fischer, 1936. $3.75.

Approved by the Paris Conservatory's Committee on Music Study.

894. Benham, Charles. Pro Art Trumpet Method. Pro Art, 1955-1957. 2 books, $2.00 each.

895. Getchell, Robert W. Practical Studies for Cornet and Trumpet. Edited by Nilo W. Hovey. Belwin-Mills, 1948. 2 books, $2.00 each.

896. Gouse, Charles F. Learn to Play the Trumpet/Cornet! (Baritone Treble Clef.) Alfred Publishing Co., 1969. 2 books, $2.50 each.

897. Gower, William and Himie Voxman. Rubank Advanced Method, Cornet or Trumpet. Rubank, 1954. V. 1, $2.50; v. 2, $3.00.

Trombones - Baritone

898. Bordner, Gerald. Practical Studies for Trombone and Baritone. Belwin-Mills, 1956-1967. 2 books, $2.00 each.

899. Cimera, Jaroslav. 221 Progressive Studies for Trombone: A Logical Volume of Supplementary Studies to Any Good Instruction Book for the Trombone. Belwin-Mills, 1942. $2.00.

900. Gouse, Charles F. Learn to Play the Trombone/Baritone! Alfred Publishing Co., 1969. 2 books, $2.50 each.

"The trombone, trumpet/cornet, and baritone books in this series may be used together with minor exceptions. These exceptions are indicated in the trombone book, at the bottom of the page where they occur.

901. Gower, William and Himie Voxman. Rubank Advanced Method, Trombone or Baritone. Rubank, 1941-1956. V. 1, $2.50; v. 2, $3.00.

902. Petrie, Charles. Pro Art Trombone and Baritone Method. Edited by Charles Benham. Pro Art, 1960-1964. 2 books, $2.00 each.

903. Rochut, Joannes, composer. <u>Melodious Etudes for</u>
      <u>Trombone</u>. Carl Fischer, 1928. 3 books, $3.00
      each.

      Transcribed from the Vocalises of Marco Bordogni
      (1788-1856), Italian singer and teacher at the
      Paris Conservatoire.

904. Tyrrell, H. W. <u>40 Progressive Studies for Trom-</u>
      <u>bone (in the Bass Clef)</u>. Boosey & Hawkes, 1954.
      $3.00.

Bass Trombone and F Attachment

905. Blume, O. <u>36 Studies for Trombone with F Attach-</u>
      <u>ment</u>. Arranged and edited by Reginald H. Fink.
      Carl Fischer, 1962. $2.50.

906. Ostrander, Allen. <u>The F Attachment and Bass Trom-</u>
      <u>bone</u>. Edited by Charles Colin. Charles Colin,
      1956. $3.50.

Tuba

907. Blazhevich, Vladislav. <u>70 Studies for BB^b Tuba</u>.
      Robert King Music Company. 2 v., $2.00 each.

908. Getchell, Robert W. <u>Practical Studies for Tuba</u>.
      Edited by Nilo W. Hovey. Belwin-Mills, 1954-1955.
      2 books, $2.00 each.

909. Gouse, Charles F. <u>Learn to Play the Tuba!</u> (BB^b
      and E^b) (Sousaphone). Alfred Publishing Co., 1970.
      2 books, $2.50 each.

910. Gower, William and Himie Voxman. <u>Rubank Advanced</u>
      <u>Method, E^b or BB^b Bass</u>. Rubank, 1951-1959. V. 1,
      $2.50; v. 2, $3.00.

911. Tyrrell, H. W. <u>Advanced Studies for B^b Bass</u>.
      Boosey & Hawkes, 1948. $3.75.

      Exercises devised by the author for those who can
      play moderately well.

PERCUSSION

Timpani

912.   Berg, Sidney. Belwin Tympani Method. Belwin-
       Mills, 1953. $2.50.

913.   Feldstein, Saul. Studies and Etudes for Timpani.
       Belwin-Mills, 1969. 3 levels, $1.50 each.

       Supplementary warm-up and technical drills,
       musicianship studies and rhythmic studies.

914.   _____. Timpani Student. Belwin-Mills, 1969.
       3 levels, $2.00 each.

915.   Firth, Vic. The Solo Timpanist: 26 Etudes. Carl
       Fischer, 1963. $3.00.

       Provides musically and technically challenging
       material for the advanced, semi-professional, or
       professional timpanist. A brief discussion of
       technical problems precedes each etude.

916.   Goodman, Saul. Modern Method for Tympani. Belwin-
       Mills, 1948. $6.00.

       4 sections: fundamentals; exercises on 2 drums;
       technique of three and more drums (including
       pedal tympani); orchestral studies and solos.

Snare Drum

917.   Albright, Fred. Contemporary Studies for Snare
       Drum. Belwin-Mills, 1966. $3.50.

       "This book contains supplementary studies at an
       advanced level expressly prepared to improve the
       sight-reading ability and technique of the per-
       cussionist who should already have knowledge of
       the rudiments of drumming."

918.   Gilbert, David W. Learn to Play the Snare and
       Bass Drum! Edited by Saul Feldstein. Alfred
       Publishing Co., 1970. $2.50.

Mallet Keyboard

919. Feldstein, Saul. Studies and Melodious Etudes
      for Mallet. Belwin-Mills, 1969. 3 levels,
      $1.50 each.

      Supplementary scales, warm-up and technical
      drills, musicianship studies, and melody-like
      studies.

920. Gilbert, David W. Learn to Play Keyboard Per-
      cussion! Edited by Sual Feldstein. Alfred
      Publishing Co., 1970. $2.50.

921. Goldenberg, Morris. Modern School for Xylophone,
      Marimba, and Vibraphone. Chappell Music Company.
      (Theodore Presser Company), 1950. $6.00.

      "With the additions of excerpts for these instru-
      ments from renowned orchestral works."

922. Schaefer, Florence. Xylophone and Marimba Method.
      Belwin-Mills, 1958. $3.00.

      Contains music theory, mallet fundamentals, marimba
      and xylophone facts, 174 short exercises, 52
      songs, and 7 music quizzes for the beginner.

Multiple Percussion

923. Burns, Roy and Saul Feldstein. Percussion Solos.
      Belwin-Mills, 1966. 3 levels (elementary, inter-
      mediate, advanced), $2.00 each.

      "Percussion solos designed to introduce the drummer
      to multiple percussion playing . . . designed to
      help him to develop the techniques necessary for
      reading contemporary percussion music."

KEYBOARD

Piano

924. Agay, Denis, ed. Technic Treasury. Warner
      Brothers. 3 books (beginner, easy, intermediate),
      $1.95 each.

925.   Clark, Frances, ed. Piano Technic. Summy-
        Birchard. 6 books, $3.95 each.

926.   Clementi, Muzio. Gradus ad Parnassum: 29
        Selected Studies. Edited by Carl Tausig.
        C. F. Peters. $10.00.

        Includes scales in thirds in all major and minor
        keys.

927.   Czerny, Carl. The Art of Finger Dexterity: Fifty
        Studies for the Piano, Op. 740. Revised and
        fingered by Max Vogrich. G. Schirmer, 1893.
        $5.00.

        Includes a biographical sketch of the composer
        by Philip Hale.

928.   _____. School of the Left Hand, Op. 399. New
        York: Franco Colombo Publications (Belwin-Mills).
        $2.75.

929.   Gold, Arthur and Robert Frizdale. Hanon Revisited:
        Contemporary Piano Exercises Based on the
        "Virtuoso Pianist."   G. Schirmer. $3.50.

930.   Hanon, Charles Lewis. The Virtuoso Pianist in 60
        Exercises. G. Schirmer, $2.50.

        "For the acquirement of agility, independence,
        strength, and perfect eveness in the fingers as
        well as suppleness of the wrist."

931.   Joseffy, Rafael. School of Advanced Piano Playing.
        G. Schirmer. $3.50.

932.   Moszkowski, Moritz. Quinze Études de virtuosité,
        Op. 72. Associated Music Publishers. $6.00.

933.   Schaum, John W. John W. Schaum Piano Course.
        Belwin-Mills. 11 books, $2.00 each.

934.   Suzuki, Shinichi. Suzuki Piano School. Summy-
        Birchard, 1970-1973. V. 1 & 2: $4.95, 12" LP,
        $8.95; V. 3 & 4: $4.95, 12" LP, $8.95; v. 5:
        $3.95; v. 6, $3.95.

935.   Thompson, John. Thompson Easiest Piano Course.
       Willis Music Company. Part 1, $.90; Parts 2-4,
       $1.00 each; Parts 5-6, $1.50 each; Parts 7-8,
       $1.00.

Organ

936.   Alcock, Walter G. The Organ. Novello, 1951.
       $8.00.

937.   Gleason, Harold. Method of Organ Playing. 5th
       edition. Appleton-Century-Crofts (Educational
       Division, Meredith Corporation), 1970. $12.95.

       Includes sections on construction and ornamentation.

938.   Hilty, Everett Jay. Principles of Organ Playing.
       Pruett Publishing Company, 1971. $10.95.

939.   Hunt, Reginald. Extemporization for Music Stu-
       dents. Oxford University Press, 1968. $5.00.

       "This course is intended first and foremost to
       help musicians to pass examination tests in this
       most difficult art."

940.   Johnson, David N. Instruction Book for Beginning
       Organists. Revised edition. Augsburg Publishing
       House, 1973. $6.95.

941.   Stainer, John. The Organ. Revised by F.
       Flaxington Harker. G. Schirmer, 1909. $2.50.

942.   Trevor, C. H. The Oxford Organ Method. Oxford
       University Press, 1971. $10.00.

       The most comprehensive organ method to have
       appeared in recent years. The practical exercises
       and examples are composed by the author and
       selected from major works in the organ repertory.
       Includes a bibliography.

GROUP INSTRUCTION

Strings

943.   Matesky, Ralph and Ralph E. Rush.   Playing and
        Teaching Stringed Instruments.   Prentice-Hall,
        1963.   Part I, $9.50.

        "Provides future instrumental teachers, parti-
        cularly those who are not string players, with
        basic instruction on how to play the violin,
        viola, cello, and string bass, and a systematic
        approach regarding organization, implementation,
        and teaching of string classes in schools."

944.   Zahtilla, Paul.   Suzuki in the String Class:
        An Adaptation of the Teachings of Shinichi
        Suzuki.   Summy-Birchard, 1972.   Teacher's manual,
        $6.00; Violin, Viola, Cello, Bass books, $2.95
        each; 4 12" LPs, $8.95 each.

Brass

945.   Winslow, Robert W. and John E. Green.   Playing and
        Teaching Brass Instruments.   Prentice-Hall, 1961.
        $7.50.

        "This book has been written for college and uni-
        versity students preparing to teach instrumental
        music in elementary and secondary schools.   It is
        designed for brass instrument classes in which
        the basic techniques of playing and teaching
        trumpet, French horn, trombone, baritone and tuba
        are presented.   The book can be used with like
        instruments or any combination of brass instruments."

GROUP TECHNICAL STUDIES

Orchestra

946.   Applebaum, Samuel.   Scales for Strings.   Belwin-
        Mills, 1962.   Books One, Two: Teacher's manual
        for each book, $3.00; Piano part for each book,
        $2.00; Violin, Viola, Cello, Bass parts for each
        book, $1.75 per part.

"To be used as supplementary studies to any
string class method or as material to develop a
string ensemble . . . Scales and arpeggios are
presented in various rhythms and bowings.

947.   Smith, Leonard B. The Treasury of Scales for
       Orchestra. Belwin-Mills, 1961. Conductor score,
       $2.00; 7 parts, $1.25 each.

948.   Waller, Gilbert R. Waller Vibrato Method for
       Strings: A Practical Approach to Vibrato
       Development for All String Players. Neil A.
       Kjos Company, 1951-1952. Violin, Viola, Cello,
       String Bass books, $1.50 each.

949.   Whistler, Harvey S. Introducing the Positions.
       Rubank, 1944-1946. V. 1: Violin-Third and Fifth
       Positions; Viola-Third and Half Positions;
       Cello-Fourth Position; $2.00 each instrument.
       V. 2: Violin-Second, Fourth, Sixth, and Seventh
       Positions; Viola-Second, Fourth, and Fifth
       Positions; Cello-Second and Third Positions;
       $2.00 (violin), $2.50 each (viola, cello).

Band

950.   Fussell, Raymonc D. Exercises for Ensemble Drill
       Arranged for Band or Orchestra. Schmitt Music
       Centers, Publications Division, 1967. $2.00.

       "A series of warming up exercises, technical
       studies, and rhythm drill for daily practice
       by any group - large or small."

951.   Smith, Leonard B. The Treasury of Scales for Band.
       Belwin-Mills, 1961. Conductor score, $3.00;
       32 parts, $1.25 each.

952.   Weber, Fred. First Division Band Method. Belwin-
       Mills, 1962-1965. Books I, II, III, IV: Conductor
       score for each book, $4.00; 18 parts for each
       book, $1.75 per part.

       "A complete curriculum of instruction and training
       for the development of an outstanding Band Program."
       (Fingering charts included in each book.)

MUSIC PUBLISHERS: THEIR ADDRESSES AND AMERICAN AGENTS

Alfred Music Company, Inc.
75 Channel Drive
Port Washington, NY 10050

AMSCO, see Oak Publications

Appleton Music Publications, see Fischer, Carl, Inc.

Ars Polana (i.e., PWM, Poland), see Marks, Edward B., Music Corp.

Artia (Czechoslovakia), see Boosey & Hawkes, Inc.

Associated Music Publishers, Inc.
866 3rd Avenue
New York, NY 10022

Augsburg Publishing House
426 South Fifth Street
Minneapolis, MN 55415

Baron, M., Co.
Box 149
Oyster Bay, NY 11771

Belwin-Mills Publishing Corp.
25 Deshon Drive
Melville, NY 11746

Big 3 Music Corp.
729 Seventh Avenue
New York, NY 10019

Boelke-Bomart Music Publications, see Schirmer, G., Inc.

Boosey & Hawkes, Inc.
30 West 57th Street
New York, NY 10019

Breitkopf & Härtel (Germany), see Associated Music Publishers or Broude, Alexander

Brodt Music Co.
1409 E. Independence Blvd.
Charlotte, NC 28201

Broude, Alexander, Inc.
225 West 57th Street
New York, NY 10019

Broude Brothers, Inc.
56 West 45th Street
New York, NY 10036

Chappell & Company, Inc.
810 Seventh Avenue
New York, NY 10019

137

Chester, J. W. (England),
see Baron, M. Co. or
Brodt Music Co.

Colin, Charles
315 West 53rd Street
New York, NY 10019

Collier Books, P. F.
(Division of Macmillan
  Publishing Co., Inc.)
866 Third Avenue
New York, NY 10022

Da Capo Press, Inc.
227 West 17th Street
New York, NY 10011

Dover Publishing Co.
180 Varick Street
New York, NY 10014

The Dulcimer Shoppe
Drawer E, Highway 9 N.
Mountain View, AK 82560

Durand & Cie, A. (France),
see Elkan-Vogel, Inc.

Elkan-Vogel, Inc.
Presser Place
Bryn Mawr, PA 19010

Eschig, Max, see
Associated Music Pub-
lishers

Eulenburg (England), see
Peters, C. F., Corporation

European American Music
  Corporation
195 Allwood Road
Clifton, NJ 07012

Foetisch (France), see
Schirmer, E. C., Music
Company

Folk-Legacy Records
Sharon Mountain Road
Sharon, CT 06069

Fischer, Carl, Inc.
56-62 Cooper Square
New York, NY 10003

Galaxy Music Corporation
2121 Broadway
New York, NY 10023

Gutheil Edition, see
Boosey & Hawkes, Inc.

Gwyn Publishing Co.
P. O. Box 5090
Sherman Oaks, CA 91413

Hansen, Wilhelm (Denmark),
see Schirmer, G., Inc.

Heugel et Cie (France),
see Presser Company, T.

International Music Co.
509 Fifth Avenue
New York, NY 10017

Kalmus, Edwin F., see
Belwin-Mills Publishing
Corp.

King, Robert, Music Co.
7 Canton Street
North Easton, MA 02356

Kjos Co., Neil A. Pub-
  lishers
4382 Jutland Drive
San Diego, CA 92117

Kneusslin (Switzerland),
see Peters, C. F.,
Corporation

Lea Pocket Scores, see
Presser Company, T.

Leduc, Alphonse (France),
see Baron, M., Co.; Brodt
Music Co.; Elkan-Vogel, Inc.

Leeds Music Corp., see
M.C.A. Music

M.C.A. Music
445 Park Avenue
New York, NY 10022

Marks, Edward B., Music
  Corp.
1790 Broadway
New York, NY 10019

Musica Rara, see Rubank,
Inc.

Novello & Company, Ltd.
1221 Avenue of the Americas
New York, NY 10020

Oak Publications
33 West 60th Street
New York, NY 10023

Oxford University Press,
  Inc.
200 Madison Avenue
New York, NY 10016

Peer International Corp.,
see Southern Music Pub.
Co., Inc.

Peters, C. F., Corporation
373 Park Avenue South
New York, NY 10016

Philharmonia Miniature
Scores (Vienna), see
European American Music
Corporation

Polskie Wydawnictwo Muzy-
czne (PWM), see Marks,
Edward B. Music Corp.

Prentice-Hall, Inc.
P. O. Box 900
Englewood Cliffs, NJ
   07631

Presser, Theodore, Co.
Presser Place
Bryn Mawr, PA 19010

Pro Art Publications, Inc.
469 Union Avenue
Westbury, NY 11590

Pruett Publishing Co.
3235 Prairie Avenue
Boulder, CO 80301

Robbins Music Corp., see
Big 3 Music Corp.

Rubank, Inc.
16215 N. W. 15th Avenue
Miami, FL 33169

Schirmer, E. C., Music
  Company
112 South Street
Boston, MA 02111

Schirmer, G., Inc.
866 3rd Avenue
New York, NY 10022

Schmidt, Oscar
Garden State Road
Union, NJ 07083

Schmitt, Hall & McCreary
  Company
Schmitt Music Centers,
Publications Division
110 North Fifth Street
Minneapolis, MN 55403

Southern Music Co.
1100 Broadway
San Antonio, TX 78206

Southern Music Pub. Co.,
  Inc.
1740 Broadway
New York, NY 10019

Stainer & Bell (England),
see Galaxy Music Corp.

Summy-Birchard Company
Evanston, IL 60204

Suvini Zerboni, Edizioni,
see Boosey & Hawkes, Inc.

TRO
10 Columbus Circle
New York, NY 10019

Universal Edition (Vienna,
London), see European
American Music Corp.

Warner Bros. Publications
  Inc.
75 Rockefeller Plaza
New York, NY 10019

Willis Music Co.
7380 Industrial Road
Florence, KY 41042

I N D E X

The index is arranged in a single alphabet and contains entries for composers as subjects, composers' works subarranged by uniform titles, authors' works subarranged by title, and distinctive titles for all listed works. The numbers refer to item numbers except in a few cases where a "p." before the number refers to a page number. Subject entries are not included other than those for composers.

ASCAP Today, 763
Aaron Copland, 696
Aaron Copland: His Life and Times, 601
Abraham, Gerald.
  BBC Music Guides, 665
Abrahams, Roger D. and George Foss.
  Anglo-American Folksong Style, 716
Academic Festival Overture, 22
Adler, Kurt.
  Operatic Anthology, 444
Advanced Studies for B♭ Bass, 911
Agay, Denes.
  Technic Treasury, 924
Aida, 485
Alban Berg: The Man & His Work, 592
Albert Herring, 455
Albright, Fred.
  Contemporary Studies for Snare Drum, 917

Alcock, Walter G.
  The Organ, 936
Allen, Reginald.
  Sir Arthur Sullivan: Composer and Personage, 649
Alphonse, Maxime.
  200 [Two Hundred] New Studies (French Horn), 887
Alte Meister des Deutschen Liedes, 434
Altenberg Lieder, 373
Alto Clarinet Student, 866
Amahl and the Night Visitors, 464
Amazing Grace and Other Gospel Sounds for Harmonica, 885
American Choral Review, 764
The American Composer Speaks, 670
American Composers on American Music, 699

The American Indians and
  Their Music, 713
The American Music Hand-
  book, 579, 680
American Music Since 1910,
  710
American Music Teacher, 765
American Musicological
  Society. Journal, 766
American Negro Folksongs,
  733
American Popular Song,
  762
American Popular Songs
  from the Revolutionary
  War to the Present,
  748
American Recorder, 767
America's Music, 671
An der schönen Blauen
  Donau, 87
The Anatomy of Jazz, 742
Ancient Voices of
  Children, 382
Andersen, Joachim.
  Twenty-four Etudes for
  the Flute, 848
Anderson, Ruth E.
  Contemporary American
  Composers, 535
Andraud, Albert J.
  Practical and Pro-
  gressive Oboe Method,
  854
Anglo-American Folksong
  Style, 716
Anthology of Italian Song
  of the 17th and 18th
  Centuries, 435
Anthony Philip Heinrich, 695
Anton Webern: An Introduction
  to His Works, 658
Antonín Dvořák, 606
Antonio Vivaldi: His Life
  and Work, 655
Apel, Willi.
  Harvard Dictionary of
  Music, 536

Appalachian Spring Suite,
  34
Applebaum, Samuel.
  The Belwin String
    Builder (Bass), 830
  The Belwin String
    Builder (Cello), 824
  The Belwin String
    Builder (Viola), 819
  The Belwin String
    Builder (Violin), 814
  Scale for Strings, 946
Arban, Joseph-Jean.
  Arban's Conservatory
    Method for Trumpet, 893
Arban's Conservatory
  Method for Trumpet, 893
Aria Albums, 443
Arnold, Denis.
  Giovanni Gabrieli, 609
  Monteverdi, 625
Arnold, Ken.
  Amazing Grace and Other
    Gospel Sounds for
    Harmonica, 885
Arnold Schoenberg: His Life,
  World and Work, 640
The Art of Finger Dex-
  terity, 927
The Art of Ragtime, 730
Artis, Bob.
  Bluegrass, 717
Austin, William W.
  "Susanna," "Jeanie," and
    "The Old Folks at Home,"
    687
'Avodat ha-kodish, 510

BBC Music Guides, 665
BMI: The Many Worlds of
  Music, 768
Bach: A Biography, 587
The Bach Family, 585
Bach, Johann Sebastian,
  586-7
  Christ lag in Todes-
    banden, 499
  Concerti grossi, 1

Bach (cont.)
  Concerto, harpsichord
    & string orchestra,
    S.1052, D minor, 2
  Concerto, violin &
    string orchestra,
    S.1041, A minor, 3
  Concerto, violin &
    string orchestra,
    S.1042, E major, 4
  Jauchzet Gott in allen
    Landen, 500
  Johannespassion, 501
  Magnificat, 502
  Mass, S.232, B minor,
    503
  Matthäuspassion, 504
  Suites, orchestra,
    S.1066-1069, 5
  Wachet auf, ruft uns
    die Stimme, 505
  Weichet nur, betrübte
    Schatten, 506
  Weihnachts-Oratorium,
    507
The Bach Reader, 586
Bachianas brasilieras,
  no. 5, 95, 427
Baerman for the Alto and
  Bass Clarinet, 865
Baermann, Karl.
  Complete Celebrated Method
    for Clarinet, 860
Baker's Biographical Dic-
  tionary of Musicians, 551
Ballad, 334
Un Ballo in Maschera, 486
Banalités, 405
Barber, Samuel.
  Songs. Selections, 370
  Summer music, 329
The Barber of Seville, 476
Il Barbiere di Siviglia,
  476
Il Barbiere di Siviglia.
  Overture, 77

Barlow, Harold.
  A Dictionary of Musi-
    cal Themes, 555
  A Dictionary of Opera
    and Song Themes, 556
The Bartered Bride, 477
Barth, Herbert, et al.
  Wagner: A Documentary
    Study, 656
Bartók, Béla, 588
  Concerto, orchestra, 6
  Contrasts, 181, 313
  Duke Bluebeard's Castle,
    449
  Music, celesta, per-
    cussion & string
    orchestra, 7
  Quartet, strings, no. 1,
    262
  Quartets, strings, 111
Barzun, Jacques.
  Berlioz and the Romantic
    Century, 593
Bass Clarinet Student, 867
Bassoon Studies, 876
Beethoven: A Documentary
  Study, 589
Beethoven, Ludwig van, 589-90
  Concerto, piano, no. 3,
    op. 37, C minor, 8
  Concerto, piano, no. 4,
    op. 58, G major, 9
  Concerto, piano, no. 5,
    op. 73, E flat major, 10
  Concerto, violin, op. 61,
    D major, 11
  Coriolan overture, 12
  Egmont. Overture, 13
  Fidelio, 450
  Leonore overture, no. 3,
    14
  Mass, op. 123, D major,
    508
  Octet, wood-winds & 2
    horns, op. 103, E^b
    major, 237, 365

Beethoven (cont.)
  Quartets, strings, 112,
    263, 308
  Quintet, piano, wood-
    winds & horn, op. 16,
    Eb major, 201, 330
  Quintet, violins, violas
    & violoncello, op. 29,
    C major, 158, 294
  Rondino, wood-winds & 2
    horns, K.25, Eb major,
    238, 366
  Septet, wood-winds, horn
    & strings, op. 20, Eb
    major, 233, 364
  Serenade, flute, violin
    & viola, op. 25, D
    major, 182, 314
  Sextet, clarinets, bas-
    soons & horns, op. 71,
    Eb major, 219, 353
  Sextet, 2 horns & strings,
    op. 81b, Eb major, 220,
    354
  Songs. Selections, 371,
    372
  Symphony, no. 3, op. 55,
    E flat major, 15
  Symphony, no. 5, op. 67,
    C minor, 16
  Symphony, no. 6, op. 68,
    F major, 17
  Symphony, no. 9, op.
    125, D minor, 18
  Trio, oboes & English
    horn, op. 87, C major,
    183, 315
  Trio, piano, clarinet
    & violoncello, op. 11,
    Bb major, 184, 316
  Trios, piano & strings,
    100, 249
  Trios, strings, 97, 246
  Works, chamber music,
    172, 244
Bellini, Vincenzo, 591
  Norma, 451

Belwin Bassoon Method, 872
Belwin Oboe Method, 855
The Belwin String Builder
  (Bass), 830
The Belwin String Builder
  (Cello), 824
The Belwin String Builder
  (Viola), 819
The Belwin String Builder
  (Violin), 814
Belwin Tympani Method, 912
Belz, Carl.
  The Story of Rock, 747
Benham, Charles.
  Pro Art Clarinet Method,
    861
  Pro Art Trumpet Method,
    894
Berg, Alban, 592
  Concerto, violin, 19
  Lyrische Suite, string
    quartet, 113
  Orchester-Lieder, Op. 4,
    373
  Quartet, strings, op. 3,
    114
  Wozzeck, 452
Berg, Sidney.
  Belwin Tympani Method,
    912
Berger, Arthur.
  Aaron Copland, 696
Berio, Luciano.
  Circles, 374
Berkowitz, Freda Pastor.
  Popular Titles and Sub-
    titles of Musical
    Compositions, 557
Berlioz and the Romantic
  Century, 593
Berlioz, Hector, 593
  La damnation de Faust,
    453
  Les nuits d'été, 375
  Requiem, 509
  Symphonie fantastique,
    20

Bertensson, Sergei.
  Sergei Rachmaninoff: A
    Lifetime in Music,
    633
Biblical Songs, 387
Bibliography of Disco-
  graphies, 561
Bibliography of North
  American Folklore and
  Folksong, 563, 714, 720
Biblische Lieder, 387
Bierley, Paul E.
  John Philip Sousa: Ameri-
    can Phenomenon, 688
  John Philip Sousa: A
    Descriptive Catalog of
    His Works, 689
The Big Bands, 745
Billboard, 769
Bio-Bibliographical Index
  of Musicians in the
  United States of America
  Since Colonial Times, 669
Biographical Dictionary of
  American Music, 672
Bizet, 594
Bizet, Georges, 594
  Carmen, 454
Black Music, 740
The Black Perspective in
  Music, 770
Blacking Up, 761
Blaukopf, Kurt.
  Mahler: A Documentary
    Study, 620
Blazhevich, Vlasislav.
  70 [Seventy] Studies for
    BBb Tuba, 907
Blesh, Rudi.
  They All Played Ragtime,
    725
Bloch, Ernest.
  'Avodat ha-kodish, 510
Blom, Eric.
  Everyman's Dictionary of
    Music, 531
The Blue Danube Waltz, 87

Bluebeard's Castle, 449
Bluegrass, 717
Blues Harmonica, 886
Blues People, 728
Blume, O.
  36 [Thirty-six] Studies
    for Trombone with F
    Attachment, 905
La Bohème, 472
Bolero, 74
Boni, Margaret Bradford.
  Fireside Book of Folk
    Songs, 445
Book of the Hanging
  Gardens, 413
The Book of World-Famous
  Music, 574
Bordner, Gerald.
  Practical Studies for
    Trombone and Bari-
    tone, 898
Boris Godunov, 470
Borodin, Aleksandr
  Porfir'evich.
  Kniaz' Igor'. Polovet-
    skaiă plîaska, 21
  Quartet, strings, no. 2,
    D major, 115, 264
Bowers, Faubion.
  The New Scriabin, 645
Bradford, Margaret.
  How to Play the Recorder,
    882
Brahms: His Life and Works,
  595
Brahms, Johannes, 595
  Akademische Festouverture,
    22
  Concerto, piano, no. 1,
    op. 15, D minor, 23
  Concerto, piano, no. 2,
    op. 83, B flat major, 24
  Concerto, violin, op. 77,
    D major, 25
  Ein deutsches Requiem, 511
  Quartets, piano & strings,
    155, 291

Brahms (cont.)
  Quartets, strings, 116,
    265
  Quintet, clarinet &
    strings, op. 115, B
    minor, 202, 331
  Quintet, piano & strings,
    op. 34, F minor, 165,
    301
  Quintet, violins, violas
    & violoncello, no. 1,
    op. 88, F major, 159,
    295
  Quintet, violins, viola
    & violoncello, no. 2,
    op. 111, G major, 160,
    296
  Sextets, violins, violas
    & violoncellos, 169,
    305
  Songs. Selections, 376
    377
  Symphony, no. 1, op. 68,
    C minor, 26
  Symphony, no. 4, op. 98,
    E minor, 27
  Trio, piano, clarinet &
    violoncello, op. 114,
    A minor, 185, 317
  Trio, piano, violin &
    horn, op. 40, Eb major,
    186, 318
  Trios, piano & strings,
    101, 250
  Variationen über ein Thema
    von Haydn, orchestra, 28
  Works, chamber music, 173,
    245
  Works, chamber music.
    Selections, 174, 309
Brandenburg Concerti, 1
Breed, Paul F.
  Songs in Collections,
    560
Brethren We Have Met, 843
Britten, 596

Britten, Benjamin, 596
  Albert Herring, 455
  A Ceremony of carols, 512
  Serenade, tenor, horn &
    string orchestra, op.
    31, 378
  The Young person's guide
    to the orchestra, 29
Brody, Elaine.
  The Music Guide to Austria
    and Germany, 571
  The Music Guide to Belgium,
    Luxembourg, Holland and
    Switzerland, 572
  The Music Guide to Great
    Britain, 570
  The Music Guide to Italy,
    573
Brook, Claire.
  The Music Guide to Austria
    and Germany, 571
  The Music Guide to Belgium,
    Luxembourg, Holland and
    Switzerland, 572
  The Music Guide to Great
    Britain, 570
  The Music Guide to Italy,
    573
Bruckner, 597
Bruckner, Anton, 597
Burns, Roy.
  Percussion Solos, 923
Byrd, William, 598
  Mass. 4 voices, 513
Byrnside, Ronald.
  Contemporary Music and
    Music Cultures, 702

Cage, John, 697, 705
  Silence: Lectures and Wri-
    tings, 697
Calvocoressi, M. C.
  Modest Mussorgsky: His Life
    and Works, 628
Canciones populares
  españolas, 388

Canteloube, Joseph.
  Chants d'Auvergne, 446
Carawan, Candy.
  Voices from the Moun-
    tains, 718
Carawan, Guy.
  Voices from the Moun-
    tains, 718
Carmen, 454
Carner, Mosco.
  Alban Berg: The Man &
    the Work, 592
  Puccini: A Critical
    Biography, 631
Carter, Elliot Cook, 701
  Etudes and a fantasy,
    wood-winds, 193, 323
  Quartet, strings, no. 1,
    117
  Quartet, strings, no. 2,
    118
  Quintet, wood-winds &
    horn, 203, 332
  Sonata, harpsichord, wood-
    winds & violoncello,
    194
Catalog of Published Concert
  Music by American Com-
  posers, 673-75
Cavalleria Rusticana, 462
Cavally, Robert, comp.
  Melodious and Progressive
    Studies for the Flute,
    849
Celebrated Arias Selected
  from Operas, 444
A Ceremony of Carols, 512
César Franck and His Circle,
  608
Chaĭkovskiĭ, Petr Il'ich,
  599
  Concerto, piano, no. 1,
    op. 23, B flat minor, 30
  Eugenii Onegen, 456
  The Nutcracker Suite, 31
  Songs. Selections, 379

Chaĭkovskiĭ (cont.)
  The Swan Lake, 32
  Symphony, no, 6, op. 74,
    B minor, 33
Chamber Music for Strings,
  174
Chamber Music of Beethoven,
  172
Chamber Music of Brahms,
  173
Chamber Music of Haydn, 175
Chamber Music of Mozart,
  178
Chamber Music of Schubert,
  179, 180
Chants d'Auverne, 446
Charles Ives and His
  America, 617, 708
Charles Ives and His
  Music, 700
Charles Ives Remembered,
  707
Charles, Sydney Robinson.
  A Handbook of Music and
    Music Literature in
    Sets and Series, 558
Chase, Gilbert.
  The American Composer
    Speaks, 670
  America's Music, 671
  The Encyclopedia of
    Opera, 548
Chausson, Ernest.
  Songs. Selections, 380
Chavez, Carlos.
  Soli, no. 2, wood-winds
    & horn, 333
La Cheminée du Roi Rene,
  343
Chopin Companion, 600
Chopin, Fryderyk Franciszek,
  600
Christ lag in Todesbanden,
  499
Christmas Oratorio, 507,
  526

Cimer, Jaroslav.
   221 [Two hundred twenty-
   one] Progressive
   Studies for Trombone,
   899
Circles, 374
The Civil War Songbook,
   690
Claghorn, Charles Eugene.
   Biographical Dictionary
   of American Music, 672
Clapham, John.
   Antonín Dvořák: Musician
   and Craftsman, 606.
Clark, Frances.
   Piano Technic, 925
Classical Symphony, 70
Clavier, 771
Clementi, Muzio
   Gradus ad Parnassum,
   926
Cobbett, W. W.
   Cobbett's Cyclopedic
   Survey of Chamber
   Music, 537
Cobbett's Cyclopedic Sur-
   vey of Chamber Music,
   537
Coker, Jerry.
   Improvising Jazz, 734
Complete Celebrated Method
   for Clarinet, 860
Concertino for String Quar-
   tet, 148
Concerto for Orchestra, 6
Contemporary American Com-
   posers, 535
Contemporary Art Song
   Album, 436
Contemporary Keyboard, 772
Contemporary Music & Music
   Cultures, 702
Contemporary Songs in
   English, 437
Contemporary Studies for
   Snare Drum, 917
Les contes d'Hoffmann, 471
Contrasts, 181, 313

Cooper, David Edwin.
   International Bibliography
   of Discographies, 559
Copland, Aaron, 601, 696
   The New Music: 1900-1960,
   698
   Appalachian spring (Suite),
   34
   Poems of Emily Dickinson,
   381
Corelli, Arcangelo.
   Concerto grosso, op. 6,
   no. 8, G minor, 35
Coriolan Overture, 12
Cosi Fan Tutti, 466
The Country Music Encyclo-
   pedia, 550
Country Music U.S.A., 755
Couperin, François, 602
Courlander, Harold.
   Negro Folk Music, U.S.A.,
   726
Cowell, Henry.
   American Composers on
   American Music, 699
   Charles Ives and His
   Music, 700
   Ballad, woodwinds &
   horn, 334
Cowell, Sidney.
   Charles Ives and His
   Music, 700
Cower, William.
   Rubank Advanced Method,
   Flute, 853
Crawford, Richard.
   The Civil War Songbook,
   690
   William Billings of
   Boston, 683
The Creation, 518
Crumb, George.
   Ancient Voices of Children,
   382
Current Musicology, 773
Czerny, Carl.
   The Art of Finger Dexterity,
   927

Czerny (cont.)
  School of the Left Hand,
    928

Dallapiccola, Luigi.
  Goethe Lieder, 383
La Damnation de Faust,
  453
Danzi, Franz.
  Quartet, bassoon &
    strings, op. 40, no.
    1, C major, 324
  Quintet, wood-winds &
    horn, op. 67, no. 2,
    E minor, 335
Daphnis et Chloe. Suite
  no. 2, 75
David, Hans T.
  The Bach Reader, 586
Davidson, James Robert.
  A Dictionary of Protes-
    tant Church Music,
    538
Davies, Laurence.
  César Franck and His
    Circle, 608
Day, James.
  Vaughan Williams, 652
De Charms, Desiree.
  Songs in Collections,
    560
Dean, Winton.
  Bizet, 594
Debussy, Claude, 603
  La Mer, 36
  Prélude à l'après-
    midi d'un faune,
    37
  Quartet, strings, op.
    10, G minor, 119,
    266
  Sonata, flute, viola &
    harp, 187
  Songs. Selections,
    384
Debussy: His Life and
  Mind, 603

Denisoff, R. Serge.
  Great Day Coming, 719
Densmore, Frances.
  The American Indians
    and Their Music, 713
Deutsch, Otto Erich.
  Mozart: A Documentary
    Biography, 626
  Schubert: A Documentary
    Biography, 641
Ein deutsches Requiem,
  511
Devienne, François.
  Quartet, bassoon &
    strings, op. 73, no.
    1, C major, 195, 325
The Diapason, 774
Dichterliebe, 418
Dictionary of Contemporary
  Music, 554
Dictionary of Hymnology,
  545
A Dictionary of Musical
  Themes, 555
A Dictionary of Opera and
  Song Themes, 556
A Dictionary of Protestant
  Church Music, 538
A Dictionary of Twentieth
  Century Composers, 553
Dido and Aeneas, 475
The Directory of Tunes and
  Musical Themes, 567
Dobrin, Arnold.
  Aaron Copland: His Life
    and Times, 601
Domenico Scarlatti, 639
Don Giovanni, 467
Don Juan, 90
Don Quichotte à Dulcinée,
  409
Donizetti and the World of
  Opera, 604
Donizetti, Gaetano, 604
  Lucia di Lammermoor, 457
Dont, Jacob.
  Etudes and Caprices for
    Violin, 815

Dotzauer, Justus.
  62 [Sixty-two] Select
    Studies for Violon-
    cello, 825
Double Canon, string quar-
  tet, 285
Dowland, John, 605
  Works. Selections; arr,
    385
Down Beat, 775
Downes, Olin.
  Treasury of American
    Song, 447
Die Dreigroschenoper,
  498
Duckles, Vincent.
  Music Reference and
    Research Materials,
    p. 73
Dukas, Paul Abraham.
  L'apprenti sorcier, 38
Duke Bluebeard's Castle,
  449
The Dulcimer Book, 847
Duparc, Henri.
  Songs. Selections, 386
Duport, Jean Louis.
  Twenty-one Etudes for
    the Violoncello, 826
Dvořák, Antonín, 606
  Biblische Lieder, 387
  Quartet, strings, B.75,
    D. minor, 120, 267
  Quartet, strings, B.92,
    Eb major, 121, 268
  Quartet, strings, B.121,
    C major, 122, 269
  Quartet, strings, B.179,
    F major, 123, 270
  Quartet, strings, B.192,
    G major, 124, 271
  Quartet, strings, B.193,
    Ab major, 125, 272
  Quintet, piano & strings,
    op. 81, A major, 166,
    302

Dvořák (cont.)
  Quintet, violins, viola,
    violoncello & double
    bass, op. 77, G major,
    162, 298
  Quintet, violins, violas
    & violoncello, op. 97,
    Eb major, 161, 297
  Symphony, no. 9, op. 95,
    E minor, 39
  Trio, piano & strings,
    no. 4, op. 90, E minor,
    102, 251

Eagon, Angelo.
  Catalog of Published Music
    by American Composers,
    673-75
Early Concert Life in
  America: 1731-1800, 685
Early Jazz, 744
Early Music, 776
Early Opera in America, 686
Edgard Varèse, 651
Edward MacDowell; A Study,
  691
Edwards, Allen.
  Flawed Words and Stubborn
    Sounds, 701
Egmont Overture, 13
Eight Etudes and a Fantasy,
  193, 323
18 [Eighteen] Selected Studies
  for Alto and Bass Clarinet,
  868
Einstein, Alfred.
  Mozart: His Character, His
    Work, 627
  Schubert: A Musical Por-
    trait, 642
Eisenhauer, William.
  Learn to Play the Clarinet!
    863
  Learn to Play the Flute!
    850

Eisenhauer (cont.)
  Learn to Play the French
    Horn!, 889
  Learn to Play the Saxo-
    phone!, 877
Elias, 520
Elijah, 520
Emperor Waltz, 89
Encyclopedia of Folk,
  Country and Western
  Music, 724
The Encyclopedia of Jazz,
  539, 735
The Encyclopedia of Jazz
  in the Seventies, 541,
  737
The Encyclopedia of Jazz
  in the Sixties, 540,
  736
The Encyclopedia of Opera,
  548
The Encyclopedia of Pop,
  Rock and Soul, 552, 760
Encyclopedia of the Musical
  Theatre, 543
Eonta, 232
Eosze, Laszol.
  Zoltán Kodály: His Life
    and Work, 618
Epstein, Dena.
  Sinful Tunes and Spirituals,
    727
Erik Satie, 638
Essays Before a Sonata,
  703
Ethnomusicology, 777
Etler, Alvin Derald.
  Quintet, brasses, 336
  Quintet, wood-winds &
    horn, no. 1, 204
  Sonic sequence, 205,
    337
Etudes and Caprices for
  Violin, 815
Eugen Onegin, 456
Everyman's Dictionary of
  Music, 531

Ewen, David.
  American Popular Songs
    from the Revolutionary
    War to the Present,
    748
  Great Men of American
    Popular Song, 749
  New Complete Book of
    the American Musical
    Theatre, 750
Exercises for Ensemble
  Drill Arranged for Band
  or Orchestra, 950
Extemporization for Music
  Students, 939
Exultate Jubilate, 521

The F Attachment and Bass
  Trombone, 906
Falla, Manuel de.
  Canciones populares
    españolas, 388
  Concerto, harpsichord,
    221
Famous Arias from Cantatas,
  Oratorios, and Operas,
  443
Farga, Franz.
  Violins and Violinists,
    660
Fauré, Gabriel Urbain, 607
  Requiem, 514
  Songs. Selections, 389
Faust, 459
Feather, Leonard.
  The Encyclopedia of Jazz,
    539, 735
  The Encyclopedia of Jazz
    in the Seventies, 541,
    737
  The Encyclopedia of Jazz
    in the Sixties, 540,
    736
Feldstein, Saul.
  Percussion Solos, 923
  Studies and Etudes for
    Timpani, 913

Feldstein (cont.)
  Studies and Melodious
    Etudes for Mallet,
    919
  Timpani Student, 914
Felix Mendelssohn & His
  Times, 622
Fellowes, Edmund H.
  William Byrd, 598
Fidelio, 450
Film Composers in America,
  754
Fine, Irving Gifford.
  Fantasia, string trio,
    247
  Partita, wood-winds &
    horn, 338
Finlandia, 84
Firebird Suite, 92
Fireside Book of Folk
  Songs, 445
First Division Band
  Method, 952
Firth, Vic.
  The Solo Timpanist:
    26 Etudes, 915
5 [Five] Greek Folk
  Songs,
Five Movements for String
  Quartet, 154, 290
Five Mystical Songs, 425
Fizdale, Robert.
  Hanon Revisited, 929
Flat-Pick Country Guitar,
  838
Flawed Words and Stubborn
  Sounds, 701
Die Fledermaus, 478
Folk Music Sourcebook,
  580, 723
The Folk Songs of North
  America, 448, 722
Folk Style Autoharp, 842
Folksingers and Folksongs
  in America, 721
Forbes, Eliot.
  Thayer's Life of Beethoven,
    590

40 [Forty] French Songs,
  438
Forty Melodic and Progressive
  Etudes for Violoncello,
  828
40 [Forty] Progressive
  Studies for Trombone, 904
40 [Forty] Songs from Eliza-
  bethan and Jacobean Song-
  books, 439
42 [Forty-two] Studies for
  Viola Solo, 821
Forty-Two Studies for
  Violin, 816
Foster, Stephen Collins, 687
  Songs. Selections, 390
Françaix, Jean.
  Quintet, wood-winds &
    horn, 206, 339
Franck, César Auguste, 608
  Symphony, D minor, 40
François Couperin and the
  French Classical Tra-
  dition, 602
Frauenliebe und Leben,
  419
Der Freischutz. Overture,
  96
French, Dorothy.
  Brethren We Have Met,
    843
Fuld, James J.
  The Book of World-
    Famous Music, 574
Fussell, Raymond C.
  Exercises for Ensemble
    Drill Arranged for Band
    or Orchestra, 950

Gabriel Fauré, 1845-1924,
  607
Gabrieli, Giovanni, 609
Galpin Society Journal, 778
Gautier, Madeline.
  Guide to Jazz, 743
Gedichte aus das Buch der
  hängenden Gärten, 413

Gedichte von Mathilde
  Wesendonck, 428
Geiringer, Karl.
  The Bach Family, 585
  Brahms: His Life and
    Works, 595
  Haydn: A Creative Life
    in Music, 613
Geistliche Lieder, 430
Gekeler, Kenneth.
  Belwin Bassoon Method,
    872
  Belwin Oboe Method,
    855
Georg Philipp Telemann,
  650
George Frederic Handel,
  612
Gerhard, Roberto.
  Quintet, wood-winds &
    horn, 207
The German Requiem, 511
Gershwin, George, 610,
  709
  Rhapsody in blue, piano
    & orchestra, 41
Gershwin: His Life and
  Music, 610, 709
Geschichte aus dem Wiener
  Wald, 88
Getchell, Robert W.
  Practical Studies for
    Cornet and Trumpet,
    895
  Practical Studies for
    French Horn, 888
  Practical Studies for
    Tuba, 908
Gibson, Gerald D.
  Bibliography of Disco-
    graphies, 561
Gilbert and Sullivan.
  See Sullivan, Sir
    Arthur Seymour
Gilbert, David W.
  Learn to Play Keyboard
    Percussion!, 920

Gilbert (cont.)
  Learn to Play the Snare
    and Bass Drum!, 918
Gillett, Charles.
  The Sound of the City,
    751
Gilman, Lawrence.
  Edward MacDowell: A
    Study, 691
Giovanni Gabrieli, 609
Girdlestone, Cuthbert.
  Jean-Philippe Rameau:
    His Life and Work,
    634
Gitler, Ira.
  The Encyclopedia of
    Jazz in the Seventies,
    541, 737
Glass, Paul.
  Singing Soldiers, 692
Gleason, Harold.
  Method of Organ Playing,
    937
  Music in America, 678
Gluck, Christoph Willi-
  bald, Ritter von.
  Orfeo ed Euridice, 458
Goethe Lieder, 383
Gold, Arthur.
  Hanon Revisited, 929
Gold, Robert.
  Jazz Talk, 542
Goldenberg, Morris.
  Modern School for Xylo-
    phone, Marimba and
    Vibraphone, 921
Goodman, Saul.
  Modern Method for
    Tympani, 916
Gotterdämmerung, 493
Gottschalk, Louis Moreau,
  693
  Notes of a Pianist, 693
Gounod, Charles Francois.
  Faust, 459
Gouse, Charles F.
  Learn to Play the Clarinet!,
    863

Gouse (cont.)
  Learn to Play the Flute!,
    850
  Learn to Play the French
    Horn!, 889
  Learn to Play the Saxo-
    phone!, 877
  Learn to Play the Trom-
    bone/Baritone!, 900
  Learn to Play the Trum-
    pet/Cornet!, 896
  Learn to Play the Tuba!,
    909
Gower, William.
  Rubank Advanced Method,
    Bassoon, 875
  Rubank Advanced Method,
    Clarinet, 864
  Rubank Advanced Method,
    Cornet or Trumpet,
    897
  Rubank Advanced Method,
    E^b or BB^b Bass, 910
  Rubank Advanced Method,
    French Horn, 890
  Rubank Advanced Method,
    Oboe, 859
  Rubank Advanced Method,
    Saxophone, 881
  Rubank Advanced Method,
    Trombone or Baritone,
    901
Gradus ad Parnassum, 926
Granados y Campiña, Enrique
  Tonadillas. Selections,
    391
Grand Collection of Scales,
    879
Grande Messe des Morts,
    509
Grauer, Bill.
  A Pictorial History of
    Jazz, 741
Gray, Michael H.
  Bibliography of Disco-
    graphies, 561

Great American Popular
  Singers, 662, 757
Great Conductors, 664
Great Day Coming, 719
Great Men of American
  Popular Song, 749
Great Singers, 663
Green, John E.
  Playing and Teaching
    Brass Instruments,
    945.
Green, Stanley.
  Encyclopedia of the
    Musical Theatre,
    543
  The World of Musical
    Comedy, 752
Grieg, 611
Grieg, Edvard Hagerup, 611
  Concerto, piano, op. 16,
    A minor, 42
  Peer Gynt (Suite), no.
    1, 43
  Peer Gynt (Suite), no.
    2, 44
  Songs. Selections, 392
Guide to Jazz, 743
A Guide to Playing the
  Recorder, 884
Guide to the Pianists'
  Repertoire, 575
Guillaume de Machaut.
  La messe de Nostre Dame,
    515
Guillaume Tell. Overture,
    78
Guitar Player, 779

H.M.S. Pinafore, 482
Hamm, Charles E.
  Contemporary Music &
    Music Cultures, 702
The Hammered Dulcimer,
    845
A Handbook of Music and
  Music Literature in
  Sets and Series, 558

Händel, Georg Friedrich,
    612
  Fireworks music, 45
  Messiah, 516
  Songs. Selections, 393
  Water music, 46
Hanon, C. L.
  The Virtuoso Pianist
    in 60 Exercises,
    930
Hanon Revisited, 929
Hansel and Gretel, 460
Harding, James.
  Erik Satie, 638
Hart, Philip.
  Orpheus in the New
    World, 676
Harvard Dictionary of
  Music, 536
Háry János Suite, 53
Havlice, Patricia Pate.
  Popular Song Index,
    562
Haydn, A Creative Life
  in Music, 613
Haydn, Joseph, 613
  Mass, D minor, 517
  Quartets, strings.
    Selections, 126,
    273
  Die Schöpfung, 518
  Songs. Selections,
    394
  Symphony, M.45, F
    sharp minor, 47
  Symphony, M.94, G
    major, 48
  Symphony, M.101,
    D major, 49
  Symphony, M.104,
    D major, 50
  Trios, piano & strings,
    103, 252
  Works, chamber music.
    Selections, 175

Haywood, Charles.
  Bibliography of North
    American Folklore and
    Folksong, 563, 714,
    720
Heinrich, Anthony Philip,
    695
Hellman, Neal.
  Life is Like a Mountain
    Dulcimer, 844
Hendrickson, Clarence V.
  Hendrickson Method for
    Clarinet, 862
Hendrickson Method for
  Clarinet, 862
Hentoff, Nat.
  The Jazz Life, 738
Henze, Hans Werner.
  Quintet, wood-winds &
    horn, 208, 340
High Fidelity/Musical
  America, 780
Hilty, Everett Jay.
  Principles of Organ
    Playing, 938
Hindemith, Paul, 614
  Kleine Kammermusik,
    wood-winds & horn,
    op. 24, no. 2, 209,
    341
  Das Marienleben (1948),
    395
  Mathis der Maler (Sym-
    phony), 51
  Octet, wood-winds, horn
    & strings, 239
  Plöner Musiktag. Mor-
    genmusik, 196, 326
  Quartet, strings, op.
    22, 127
  Symphonic metamorphosis
    of themes by Carl Maria
    Von Weber, 52
Hinson, Maurice.
  Guide to the Pianists'
    Repertoire, 575

Historia von der Geburt
  Jesu Christi, 526
A History of Popular Music
  in America, 759
Hitchcock, H. Wiley.
  Ives, 616
  Music in the United
    States, 677
Hodeir, André.
  Jazz: Its Evolution
    and Essence, 739
Hodie, 528
Holden, Sally.
  Life is Like a Mountain
    Dulcimer, 844
Holst, Gustav, 615
Holst, Imogen.
  Britten, 596
  The Music of Gustav
    Holst, 615
Honegger, Arthur.
  Le roi David, 519
Horn, David.
  The Literature of Ameri-
    can Music, 564, p. 95
Horton, John.
  Grieg, 611
Household Songs, 390
How to Play the 5-string
  Banjo, 840
How to Play the Recorder,
  882
Hugo Wolf: A Biography,
  659
Humperdinck, Engelbert.
  Hansel und Gretel, 460
Hunt, Reginald.
  Extemporization for Music
    Students, 939

Ibert, Jacques.
  Pièces brèves, wood-winds
    & horn, 210, 342
Improvising Jazz, 634
In Memoriam Dylan Thomas,
  422
Information on Music, p. 73

Institute for Studies in
  American Music. News-
  letter, 781
Instruction Book for Be-
  ginning Organists, 940
Instrumental Techniques
  of American Folk
  Guitar, 836
Instrumentalist, 782
International Basic List
  of Literature on Music,
  p. 73
International Bibliography
  of Discographies, 559
International Cyclopedia of
  Music and Musicians, 534
International Folk Music
  Council. Yearbook, 783
International Repertory of
  Music Literature, 568
International Who's Who
  in Music, 544
Introducing the Alto or
  Bass Clarinet, 871
Introducing the Positions,
  949
Introduction et allegro,
  234
Ives, 616
Ives, Charles Edward, 616-17,
  700, 703, 704, 707, 708
  Essays Before a Sonata,
    703
  Largo, piano, clarinet,
    violin, 319
  Memos, 704
  Quartet, strings, no. 1,
    128, 274
  Quartet, strings, no. 2,
    129, 275
  Songs, 396
  Trio, piano & strings,
    253

Jackson, Richard.
  United States Music, p. 95

Jacob, Heinrich E.
  Felix Mendelssohn & His
    Times, 622
Jacobs, Frederick.
  Learn to Play the Clari-
    net!, 863
  Learn to Play the Flute!,
    850
  Learn to Play the Saxo-
    phone, 877
Janáček, Leoš.
  Mládí, 222, 355
  Quartet, strings, no. 2,
    130
Janis, Harriet.
  They All Played Ragtime,
    725
Jauchzet Gott in allen
  Landen, 500
Jazz: A History, 746
Jazz Guitar Method, 833
Jazz: Its Evolution and
  Essence, 739
The Jazz Life, 738
Jazz Talk, 542
Jean-Philippe Rameau: His
  Life and Work, 634
Johannespassion, 501
John Cage, 705
John Dowland: His Life and
  Works, 605
John Philip Sousa: Ameri-
  can Phenomenon, 688
John Philip Sousa: A Des-
  criptive Catalog of His
  Works, 689
John W. Schaum Piano Course,
  933
Johnson, David N.
  Instruction Book for Be-
    ginning Organists,
    940
Johnson, Robert Sherlaw.
  Messiaen, 623
Jones, LeRoi.
  Black Music, 740
  Blues People, 728

Joseffy, Rafael.
  School of Advanced Piano
    Playing, 931
Journal of Band Research,
  784
Journal of Church Music,
  785
Journal of Country Music,
  786
Journal of Jazz Studies,
  787
Journal of Music Theory,
  788
Journal of Music Therapy,
  789
Journal of Research in
  Music Education, 790
Julian, John.
  Dictionary of Hymnology,
    545

Kaiser-Walzer, 89
Kallin, Anna.
  Twentieth-Century Com-
    posers, 666
Kayser, Heinrich Ernest.
  36 [Thirty-six] Studies
    (Elementary and Pro-
    gressive) for Viola
    Solo, 820
Keepnews, Orrin.
  A Pictorial History of
    Jazz, 741
Keil, Charles.
  Urban Blues, 729
Kennedy, Michael.
  Richard Strauss, 647
Kindertotenlieder, 398
Kirkpatrick, Ralph.
  Domenico Scarlatti, 639
Kleine Kammermusik, 209,
  341
Eine kleine Nachtmusik, 133
Klengel, Julius.
  Technical Studies for the
    Violoncello, 827

Kobbé's Complete Opera Book,
    576
Kodály, Zoltán, 618
    Háry János. Suite, 53
Koechlin, Charles L.
    Gabriel Fauré, 1845-1924,
    607
Kolneder, Walter.
    Anton Webern: An Intro-
    duction to His Works,
    658
    Antonio Vivaldi: His Life
    and Work, 655
Kostelanetz, Richard.
    John Cage, 705
Krasilousky, William.
    More About This Business
    of Music, 582
    This Business of Music,
    581
Kreutzer, Rodolphe.
    42 [Forty-two] Studies
    for Viola Solo, 821
    Forty-two Studies for
    Violin, 816
Kulbach, Johanna.
    The Recorder Guide, 883

La Grange, Henry-Louis de.
    Mahler, 621
Labanchi, Gaetano.
    Thirty-Three Concert
    Etudes, 878
Landon, Grelun.
    Encyclopedia of Folk,
    Country and Western
    Music, 724
Landon, H. C. Robbins.
    Beethoven: A Documentary
    Study, 589
Lang, Paul Henry.
    George Frederic Handel,
    612
Langsamer Satz, 151, 288
Largo for Violin, Clarinet
    & Piano, 319
Lawless, Ray M.
    Folksingers and Folksongs
    in America, 721

Layton, Robert.
    Sibelius, 644
Learn to Play the Clarinet!,
    863
Learn to Play the Flute!,
    850
Learn to Play the French
    Horn!, 889
Learn to Play the Keyboard
    Percussion!, 920
Learn to Play the Oboe!,
    856
Learn to Play the Saxo-
    phone!, 877
Learn to Play the Snare
    and Bass Drum!, 918
Learn to Play the Trombone/
    Baritone!, 900
Learn to Play the Trumpet/
    Cornet!, 896
Learn to Play the Tuba,
    909
Lee, Sebastian.
    Forty Melodic and Pro-
    gressive Etudes for
    Violoncello, 828
Leoncavallo, Ruggiero.
    I Pagliacci, 461
Leonore Overture, 14
Lewine, Richard.
    Songs of the American
    Theater, 565, 753
Leyda, Jay.
    Sergei Rachmaninoff: A
    Lifetime in Music, 633
Lichtenwanger, William.
    A Survey of Musical
    Instrument Collections,
    577
Lieder eines fahrenden
    Gesellen, 400
Liederkreis, 420
The Life and Music of Béla
    Bartók, 588
Life is Like a Mountain
    Dulcimer, 844
A List of Books on Music,
    p. 85
Liszt, 619

Liszt, Franz, 619
  Concerto, piano, no. 1,
    E flat major, 54
  Les Preludes, 55
  Songs. Selections, 397
The Literature of American
  Music, 564, p. 95
Lockspeiser, Edward.
  Debussy: His Life and
    Mind, 603
Loesser, Arthur.
  Men, Women and Pianos,
    661
Lohengrin, 492
Lomax, Alan.
  The Folk Songs of North
    America, 448, 722
Lowens, Irving.
  Music and Musicians in
    Early America, 682
Lucia di Lammermoor, 457
Lutoslawski, Witold.
  Quartet, strings, 131
Lyrische Suite, string
  quartet, 113

Má vlast. Vltava, 86
MacBeth, James.
  Learn to Play the Oboe!,
    856
McCarty, Clifford.
  Film Composers in
    America, 754
MacDowell, Edward Alex-
  ander, 691
McDowell, Paul D.
  Practical Studies for
    Bassoon, 873
McKay, David.
  William Billings of
    Boston, 683
McSpadden, Lynn.
  Brethren We Have Met,
    843
Madama Butterfly, 473
The Magic Flute, 469
Magnificat, 502

Mahler, 621
Mahler: A Documentary Study,
  620
Mahler, Gustav, 620-21
  Kindertotenlieder, 398,
    399
  Lieder eines fahrenden
    Gesellen, 56, 400
  Symphony, no. 2, C
    minor, 57
  Symphony, no. 4, G
    major, 58
Malone, Bill C.
  Country Music U.S.A.,
    755
Manon, 463
The Many Ways to Play the
  Autoharp, 841
Marco, Guy.
  Information on Music,
    p. 73
Marcuse, Sibyl.
  Musical Instruments, 546
  A Survey of Music Instru-
    ments, 578
Das Marien Leben, 395
The Marriage of Figaro, 468
Marrocco, W. Thomas.
  Music in America, 678
Mascagni, Pietro.
  Cavalleria rusticana,
    462
The Masked Ball, 486
Mason, Colin.
  Oxford Studies of Com-
    posers, 667
Mass in B minor, 503
Massenet, Jules Émile
  Frédéric.
  Manon, 463
The Master Musicians
  Series, 597, 611, 628,
    632, 647, 652, 668
Matesky, Ralph.
  Playing and Teaching
    Stringed Instruments,
    943

Mathis der Maler, 51
Mattfeld, Julius.
  Variety Music Caval-
    cade 1620-1969, 583,
    756
Matthäuspassion, 504
Mayeur, L.
  Grand Collection of
    Scales, 879
Mazas, Jacques Féréol.
  30 [Thirty] Etudes Spé-
    ciales for Viola Solo,
    822
  26 [Twenty-six] Etudes
    Brilliantes for Viola
    Solo, 823
Die Meistersinger von
  Nürnberg, 491
Mellers, Wilfred H.
  Francois Couperin and the
    French Classical Tra-
    dition, 602
Mellers, Wilfrid.
  Music in a New Found Land,
    679
Melodies populaires grecques,
  410
Melodious and Progressive
  Studies for Flute, 849
Melodious Etudes for Trom-
  bone, 903
Memos, 704
Men, Women and Pianos, 661
Mendel, Arthur.
  The Bach Reader, 586
Mendelssohn-Bartholdy, Felix,
  622
  Concerto, violin, op. 64,
    E minor, 59
  Elias, 520
  Octet, 4 violins, 2 violas
    & 2 violoncellos, op.
    20, Eb major, 170, 306
  Quartets, strings, 132,
    276
  Ein Sommernachtstraum,
    op. 61, 60
  Ein Sommernachtstraum.
    Overture, op. 21, 61

Mendelssohn-Bartholdy (cont.)
  Symphony, no. 4, op. 90,
    A major, 62
  Trios, piano & strings,
    104, 254
  Works, chamber music.
    Selections, 176
Menotti, Gian Carlo.
  Amahl and the night
    visitors, 464
La Mer, 36
La Messe de Nostre Dame, 515
Messiaen, 623
Messiaen, Oliver, 623
  Quatuor pour la fin du
    temps, 327
The Messiah, 516
Method for the Spanish
  Guitar, 835
Method of Organ Playing,
  937
Midsummer Night's Dream, 60
Midsummer Night's Dream.
  Overture, 61
The Mikado, 483
Milde, Ludwig.
  25 [Twenty-five] Studies
    in Scales and Chords
    for Bassoon, op. 24
    874
Milhaud, Darius, 624
  La cheminée du roi Rene,
    343
  Notes without Music: An
    Autobiography, 624
Miscellaneous Chamber
  Works, 177
Missa Papae Marcelli, 523
Mitchell, Howard W.
  The Hammered Dulcimer,
    845
  The Mountain Dulcimer,
    846
Mládí, 222, 355
Modern Method for Tympani,
  916
Modern School for Xylo-
  phone, Marimba and Vibra-
  phone, 921

Modern Music: A Quarterly
  Review, 706
Modest Mussorgsky: His
  Life and Works, 628
The Moldau, 86
Monteverdi, 625
Monteverdi, Claudio, 625
  L'Orfeo, 465
Montgomery, Wes.
  Jazz Guitar Method, 833
More About This Business
  of Music, 582
Morgan, Tommy.
  Blues Harmonica, 886
Morgenmusik, 196, 326
Morgenstern, Sam.
  A Dictionary of Musical
    Themes, 555
  A Dictionary of Opera
    and Song Themes, 556
Moszkowski, Moritz.
  Quinze Études de vir-
    tuosité, 932
The Mountain Dulcimer,
  846
Mozart: A Documentary
  Biography, 626
Mozart: His Character, His
  Work, 627
Mozart, Johann Chrysostom
  Wolfgang Amadeus, 626-27
  Concerto, piano, K.466,
    D minor, 63
  Concerto, piano, K.488,
    A major, 64
  Cosi fan tutti, 466
  Divertimento, K.213, F
    major, 223, 356
  Divertimento, K.240,
    B^b major, 224, 357
  Divertimento, K.240a,
    (252) E^b major, 225,
    358
  Divertimento, K.253, F
    major, 226, 359
  Divertimento, K.270,
    B^b major, 227, 360

Mozart (cont.)
  Divertimento, K.271b
    (287), B^b major, 228
  Divertimento, K.271g
    (289), E^b major, 361
  Divertimento, string
    trio, K.563, E^b
    major, 98, 248
  Don Giovanni, 467
  Exultate jubilate, 521
  Eine kleine Nachtmusik,
    65, 133
  Ein musikalischer Spass,
    229, 362
  Le nozze di Figaro,
    468
  Quartet, flute & strings,
    K.285, D major, 197
  Quartet, flute & strings,
    K.285a, G major, 198
  Quartet, flute & strings,
    K.298, A major, 199
  Quartet, oboe & strings,
    K.368b (370), F major,
    200
  Quartets, flute & strings,
    328
  Quartets, piano & strings,
    156, 292
  Quartets, strings, 277,
    310
  Quartets, strings. Selec-
    tions, 134
  Quintet, clarinet &
    strings, K.581, A major,
    211, 344
  Quintet, horn & strings,
    K.386c (407), E^b major,
    212, 345
  Quintet, piano, wood-
    winds & horn, K.452,
    E^b major, 213, 346
  Quintets, violins, violas
    & violoncello, 163,
    299
  Requiem, 522

Mozart (cont.)
  Serenade, wood-winds & 2
    horns, K.375, E flat
    major, 240, 367
  Songs. Selections, 401,
    402
  Symphony, K.504, D
    major, 66
  Symphony, K.550, G
    minor, 67
  Symphony, K.551, C
    major, 68
  Trio, piano, clarinet
    & viola, K.498, E^b
    major, 188, 320
  Trios, piano & strings,
    105, 255
  Works, chamber music.
    Selections, 177
  Zauberflöte, 469
Music and Letters, 791
Music and Musicians in
  Early America, 682
Music Educator's Journal,
  792
Music for Strings, Per-
  cussion and Celesta,
  7
The Music Guide to Aus-
  tria and Germany, 571
The Music Guide to Bel-
  gium, Luxembourg,
  Holland and Switzer-
  land, 572
The Music Guide to Great
  Britain, 570
The Music Guide to
  Italy, 573
Music in a New Found
  Land, 679
Music in America, 678
Music in the Cultured
  Generation, 694
Music in the United
  States, 677
Music Index, 566
Music Journal, 793

Music Journal Annual;
  Anthology, 794
Music Library Association,
  Notes, 795
The Music of Black
  Americans, 731
The Music of Gustav
  Holst, 615
Music of the Moravians
  in America, 440
The Music of the Pil-
  grims, 684
Music Reference and Re-
  search Materials,
  p. 73
Music Review, 796
Music Since 1900, 584
Musical America: Inter-
  national Directory of
  the Performing Arts,
  797
Musical Instruments: A
  Comprehensive Dic-
  tionary, 546
Musical Instruments of
  the World, 547
Musical Joke, 229, 362
Musical Quarterly, 798
Musical Times, 799
Ein musikalischer Spass,
  229, 362
Musorgskiĭ, Modest
  Petrovich, 628
  Boris Godunov, 470
  The Nursery, 403
  Pictures at an exhi-
    bition; arr., 69
  Songs and dances of
    death, 404
Mussulman, Joseph A.
  Music in the Cultured
    Generation, 694
My Musical Life, 636

Nabokov, Nicholas.
  Twentieth-Century Com-
    posers, 666

National Association of
Teachers of Singing.
Bulletin, 800
National Music Council.
Bulletin, 801
Negro Folk Music, U.S.A.,
726
Nelson Mass, 517
Nestyev, Israel.
Prokofiev, 630
Nettl, Bruno.
Contemporary Music &
Music Cultures, 702
North American Indian
Musical Styles, 715
New Complete Book of the
American Musical Theatre,
750
The New Grove Dictionary
of Music and Musicians,
532
New Methods for the
Double Bass, 831
The New Music: 1900-1960.
698
The New Scriabin, 645
Newman, Ernest.
Wagner as Man and Artist,
657
Nielsen, Carl.
Quartet, strings, no. 4,
op. 44, F major, 135,
278
Quintet, wood-winds &
horn, op. 43, 214,
347
19th-Century Music, 802
Nitka, Arthur.
The Recorder Guide, 883
Noad, Frederick M.
Solo Guitar Playing, 834
Norma, 451
North American Indian
Musical Styles, 715
Notes of a Pianist, 693
Notes without Music, 624
Le Nozze di Figaro, 468

Les nuits d'été, 375
The Nursery, 403
Nutcracker Suite, 31

Octandre, 243
Offenbach, Jacques.
Les contes d'Hoffmann,
471
L'oiseau de feu, 92
Old-time Mountain Banjo,
839
Opera News, 803
Operatic Anthology, 444
Orchester-Lieder, 373
Orenstein, Arbie.
Ravel: Man and Musician
635
L'Orfeo, 465
Orfeo ed Euridice, 458
The Organ, 936, 941
Orpheus in the New World,
676
Orrey, Leslie.
The Encyclopedia of
Opera, 548
Ostransky, Leroy.
The Anatomy of Jazz,
742
Ostrander, Allen.
The F Attachment and Bass
Trombone, 906
Otello, 487
Ouellete, Fernard.
Edgard Varèse, 651
The Oxford Companion to
Music, 533
The Oxford Organ Method,
942
Oxford Studies of Composers,
616, 629, 667

I Pagliacci, 461
Palestrina, 629
Palestrina, Giovanni, 629
Missa Pape Marcelli, 523
Panassie, Hugues.
Guide to Jazz, 743

Parker, Elizabeth.
How to Play the Re-
corder, 882
Parsons, Denys. The
Directory of Tunes and
Musical Themes, 567
Paul Hindemith: The Man
Behind the Music, 614
Pavlakis, Christopher.
The American Music Hand-
book, 579, 680
Pease, Donald J.
Pro Art Flute and
Piccolo Method, 851
Pro Art French Horn
Method in F and F♭,
891
Pro Art Saxophone
Method, 880
Peer Gynt Suite No. 1, 43
Peer Gynt Suite No. 2, 44
Penderecki, Krzysztof.
Quartet, strings, no.
1, 136
Percussion Solos, 923
Pergolesi, Giovanni
Battista.
Stabat Mater, 524
Perlis, Vivian.
Charles Ives Remembered,
707
Perspectives of New
Music, 804
Peter and the Wolf, 71
Petrie, Charles.
Pro Art French Horn
Method in F and F♭,
891
Pro Art Trombone and
Baritone Method, 902
Peterson, Meg.
The Many Ways to Play
the Autoharp, 841
Petroushka, 93
Petzoldt, Richard.
Georg Philipp Telemann,
650
Piano Technic, 925

Pickin', 805
A Pictorial History of
Jazz, 741
Pictures at an Exhibition, 69
Pièces brèves, wood-winds
& horn, 210 342
Pinafore, 482
The Pirates of Penzance, 484
Piston, Walter.
Pieces, flute, clarinet
& bassoon, 189, 321
Playing and Teaching Brass
Instruments, 945
Playing and Teaching
Stringed Instruments, 943
Pleasants, Henry.
Great Singers, 663
Great American Popular
Singers, 662, 757
Plöner Musiktag. Morgen-
musik, 196, 326
Poems of Emily Dickinson, 381
Poems of Love and the
Rain, 411
Poerter, Neal.
Alto Clarinet Student, 866
Polovetsian Dances, 21
Popular Music, 758
Popular Music and Society,
806
Popular Song Index, 562
Popular Titles and Sub-
titles of Musical Com-
positions, 557
Pottag, Max P.
Preparatory Melodies to
Solo Work for French
Horn, 892
Poulenc, Francis.
Banalités, 405
Sextet, piano, wood-winds
& horn, 230, 363
Sonata, trumpet, horn &
trombone, 190, 322
Poulton, Diana.
John Dowland: His Life
and Works, 605

Practical and Progressive
  Oboe Method, 854
Practical Studies for
  Bassoon, 873
Practical Studies for
  Cornet and Trumpet,
  895
Practical Studies for
  French Horn, 888
Practical Studies for
  Trombone and Baritone,
  898
Practical Studies for
  Tuba, 908
Pratt, Waldo S.
  The Music of the Pil-
    grims, 684
Prélude à l'après-midi
  d'un faune, 37
Les Preludes, 55
Preparatory Melodies to
  Solo Work for French
  Horn, 892
Prince Igor. Polovet-
  sian Dances, 21
Principles of Organ Playing,
  938
Pro Art Clarinet Method,
  861
Pro Art Flute and Piccolo
  Method, 851
Pro Art French Horn Method
  in F and E^b, 891
Pro Art Saxophone Method,
  880
Pro Art Trombone and Bari-
  tone Method, 902
Pro Art Trumpet Method,
  894
Prodaná nevěsta, 477
Prokof'ev, Sergeĭ Sergeevich,
  630
  Classical symphony, 70
  Peter and the Wolf, 71
  Quartet, strings, no. 1,
    op. 50, 137, 279

Prokof'ev (cont.)
  Quartet, strings, no. 2,
    op. 92, 138, 280
  Quintet, oboe, clarinet
    & strings, op. 39,
    215, 348
  Le vilain petit canard, 406
Prokofiev, 630
Protestant Church Music in
  America, 681
Public Libraries Commission
  of the International Asso-
  ciation of Music Libraries.
  International Basic List
  of Literature on Music,
  p. 85
Puccini: A Critical Bio-
  graphy, 631
Puccini, Giacomo, 631
  La Bohème, 472
  Madama Butterfly, 473
  Tosca, 474
Purcell, 632
Purcell, Henry, 632
  Dido and Aeneas, 475
  Songs. Selections, 407

Quartetti concertanti, 195,
  325
Quatuor pour la fin du
  temps, 327
Quinze Études de vir-
  tuosité, 932

RILM Abstracts of Musical
  Literature, 568
Rachmaninoff, Sergei, 633
  Concerto, piano, no. 2,
    op. 18, c minor, 72
  Rapsodie sur un thème
    de Paganini, piano and
    orchestra, 73
  Songs. Selections, 408
The Rake's Progress, 481
Rameau, Jean Philippe, 634
Ravel: Man and Musician,
  635

Ravel, Maurice, 635
  Bolero, orchestra,
    74
  Daphnis et Chloe, Suite
    no. 2, 75
  Don Quichotte à Dulcinée,
    409
  Introduction et allegro,
    harp, wood-winds &
    strings, 234
  Melodies populaires
    grecques, 410
  Quartet, strings, F
    major, 139, 281
  Trio, piano & strings,
    A minor, 106, 256
Readings in Black American
  Music, 732
The Recorder Guide, 883
Records and Recordings,
  807
Reger, Max.
  Serenade, flute, violin &
    viola, op. 77a, D major,
    191
  Serenade, flute, violin &
    viola, op. 141a, G major,
    192
Reicha, Anton Joseph.
  Quintet, wood-winds & horn,
    op. 91, no. 1, C major,
    349
  Quintet, wood-winds & horn,
    op. 100, no. 4, E minor,
    350
Rhapsody in Blue, 41
Rhapsody on a Theme of
  Paganini, 73
Das Rheingold, 494
Rhoads, William E.
  Baermann for the Alto
    and Bass Clarinet,
    865
  18 [Eighteen] Selected
    Studies for Alto and
    Bass Clarinet, 868
  35 [Thirty-five] Technical
    Studies for Alto and Bass
    Clarinet, 869

Rhoads (cont.)
  21 [Twenty-one] Foundation
    Studies for Alto and
    Bass Clarinet, 870
Rich, Maria F.
  Who's Who in Opera, 549
Richard Strauss, 647
Riedel, Johannes.
  The Art of Ragtime, 730
Rigoletto, 488
Rimskiĭ-Korsakov, Nikolaĭ
    Andreevich, 636
  My Musical Life, 636
  Scherherazade, 76
Der Ring des Nibelungen,
    493-96
Ritchie, Jean.
  The Dulcimer Book, 847
Robert Schumann: The Man
  and His Music, 643
Rochberg, George.
  Serenata d'estate, 231
Roche, Jerome.
  Palestrina, 629
Rochut, Joannes.
  Melodious Etudes for
    Trombone, 903
Le Roi David, 519
Rolling Stone, 808
Rorem, Ned.
  Poems of Love and the
    Rain, 411
  Visits to St. Elizabeth's,
    412
Rosenbaum, Art.
  Old-time Mountain Banjo,
    839
Der Rosenkavalier, 479
Rossini: A Biography, 637
Rossini, Gioacchino Antonio,
    637
  Il barbiere di Siviglia,
    476
  Il barbiere di Siviglia.
    Overture, 77
  Guillaume Tell. Over-
    ture, 78
Rossiter, Frank R.
  Charles Ives and His
    America, 617, 708

Royal Fireworks Music, 45
Rubank Advanced Method,
Bassoon, 875
Rubank Advanced Method,
Clarinet, 864
Rubank Advanced Method,
Cornet or Trumpet, 897
Rubank Advanced Method,
E♭ or BB♭ Bass, 910
Rubank Advanced Method,
Flute, 853
Rubank Advanced Method,
French Horn, 890
Rubank Advanced Method,
Oboe, 859
Rubank Advanced Method,
Saxophone, 881
Rubank Advanced Method,
Trombone or Baritone,
901
Rush, Ralph E.
Playing and Teaching
Stringed Instruments,
943

Le sacre du printemps,
94
Sacred Service, 510
Sadie, Stanley.
The New Groves Dic-
tionary of Music and
Musicians, 532
Sätze, string quartet,
154, 290
St. Matthew Passion, 504
St. John Passion, 501
Salome, 480
Sandberg, Larry.
Folk Music Sourcebook,
580, 723
Satie, Eric, 638
Sato Cello School, 829
Scales for Strings, 946
Scarlatti, Domenico, 639
Schaefer, Florence.
Xylophone and Marimba
Method, 922

Schafer, William J.
The Art of Ragtime, 730
Schaum, John W.
John W. Schaum Piano
Course, 933
Scheherazade, 76
Schönberg, Arnold, 640
Gedichte aus das Buch
der hängenden Gärten,
413
Quartet, strings, no.
1, op. 7, D minor,
140
Quartet, strings, no.
2, op. 10, F# minor,
141
Quartet, strings, no.
3, op. 30, 142
Quartet, strings, no.
4, op. 37, 143
Quintet, wood-winds &
horn, op. 26, 216
Suite, piano, 3 clari-
nets & strings, op.
29, 235
Trio, strings, op. 45,
99
Verklärte Nacht, 79,
171, 307
Die Schöne Mullerin, 414
Die Schöpfung, 518
Scholes, Percy A.
The Oxford Companion to
Music, 533
Schonberg, Harold.
Great Conductors, 664
School of Advanced Piano
Playing, 931
School of the Left Hand,
928
Schubert: A Documentary
Biography, 641
Schubert: A Musical Por-
trait, 642
Schubert, Franz Peter, 641-42
Adagio, piano trio, D.897,
E♭ major, 257

Schubert (cont.)
 Chamber music. Selec-
  tions, 180
 Mass, D.167, G major,
  525
 Octet, winds & strings,
  D.803, F major, 241,
  368
 Quartets, strings,
  144
 Quartets, strings.
  Selections, 282
 Quintet, piano, violin,
  viola, violoncello,
  & double bass, D.667,
  A major, 167, 303
 Quintet, violins, viola,
  & violoncellos, D.956,
  C major, 164, 300
 Die Schöne Mullerin,
  414
 Schwanengesang, 415
 Songs. Selections, 416
 Symphony, D.759, B
  minor, 80
 Trios, piano & strings,
  107, 258
 Die Winterreise, 417
 Works, chamber music,
  179, 311, 312
Schuller, Gunther.
 Early Jazz, 744
 Quintet, wood-winds &
  horn, 217, 351
Schumann, Robert Alexander,
  643
 Concerto, piano, op. 54,
  A minor, 81
 Dichterliebe, 418
 Frauenliebe und Leben,
  419
 Liederkreis, op. 24,
  420
 Quartet, piano & strings,
  op. 47, E^b major,
  157, 293
 Quartets, strings, 145,
  283

Schumann (cont.)
 Quintet, piano & strings,
  op. 44, E^b major, 168,
  304
 Symphony, no. 3, op. 97,
  E flat major, 82
 Trios, piano & strings,
  108, 259
Schütz, Heinrich.
 Historia von der Geburt
  Jesu Christi, 526
Schwanengesang, 415
Schwann Record & Tape
 Guide, 569
Schwartz, Charles.
 Gershwin: His Life and
  Music, 610, 709
Seeger, Peter.
 How to Play the 5-String
  Banjo, 840
Selected Studies for
 Flute, 852
Selected Studies for
 Oboe, 858
Sergei Rachmaninoff: A
 Lifetime in Music, 633
Serenade for Tenor, Horn,
 and Strings, 378
Serenata d'estate, 231
Seven Popular Spanish
 Songs, 388
70 [Seventy] Studies for
 BB^b Tuba, 907
Shapiro, Nat.
 Popular Music, 758
Shemel, Sidney M.
 More About This Busi-
  ness of Music, 582
 This Business of
  Music, 581
Shestack, Melvin.
 The Country Music En-
  cyclopedia, 550
Shostakovich, Dmitriĭ
 Dmitrievich.
 Quartet, strings, no.
  1, E minor, 146

Shostakovich (cont.)
  Symphony, no. 5, op.
    47, 83
  Trio, piano & strings,
    no. 2, op. 67, E
    minor, 109, 260
Sibelius, 644
Sibelius, Jean, 644
  Finlandia, 84
  Symphony, no. 2, op.
    43, 85
Siegfried, 495
Silence: Lectures and
  Writings, 697
Simandl, Franz.
  New Method for the
    Double Bass, 831
  Thirty Etudes, 832
Simon, Alfred.
  Songs of the American
    Theater, 565, 753
Simon, George.
  The Big Bands, 745
Sinful Tunes and Spiri-
  tuals, 727
Sing Out!, 809
Singing Soldiers, 692
Sir Arthur Sullivan: Com-
  poser and Personage, 649
Six Bagatelles for String
  Quartet, 150, 287
Sixty Etudes for Violin,
  818
62 [Sixty-two] Select Stu-
  dies for Violoncello, 825
Skelton, Geoffrey.
  Paul Hindemith: The Man
    Behind the Music, 614
Skriabin, Aleksandr Niko-
  laevich, 645
Slonimsky, Nicolas.
  Baker's Biographical
    Dictionary of Musicians,
    551
  Music Since 1900, 584
Slow Movement for Quartet,
  151, 288

Smetana, Bedřich.
  Má Vlast. Vltava, 86
  Prodana nevesta, 477
  Quartet, strings, no. 1,
    E minor, 147, 284
  Trio, piano & strings,
    op. 15, G minor, 110,
    261
Smith, Leonard B.
  The Treasury of Scales
    for Band, 951
  The Treasury of Scales
    for Orchestra, 947
Soli, no. 2, wood-winds &
  horn, 333
Solo Guitar Playing, 834
The Solo Timpanist: 26
  Etudes, 915
Ein Sommernachtstraum, 60
Ein Sommernachtstraum.
  Overture, 61
Song and Dances of Death, 404
Songs by 22 Americans, 441
Songs from William Blake,
  424
Songs in Collections, 560
Songs of a Wayfarer, 56, 400
Songs of the American
  Theater, 565, 753
Songs of Travel, 426
Sonic Sequence, 205, 337
Sonneck, Oscar G.
  Early Concert Life in
    America: 1731-1800, 685
  Early Opera in America,
    686
Sor, Ferdinand.
  Method for the Spanish
    Guitar, 835
The Sorcerer's Apprentice, 38
The Sound of the City, 751
Sousa, John Philip, 688-89
Southern, Eileen.
  The Music of Black Ameri-
    cans, 731
  Readings in Black Ameri-
    can Music, 732

Spaeth, Sigmund.
  A History of Popular
    Music in America,
    759
Spanish Songs of the 18th
  Century, 442
Stabat Mater, 524
Stainer, John.
  The Organ, 941
Stambler, Irwin.
  Encyclopedia of Folk,
    Country and Western
    Music, 724
  The Encyclopedia of Pop,
    Rock and Soul, 552,
    758
Stereo Review, 810
Stevens, Halsey.
  The Life and Music of
    Béla Bartók, 588
Stevenson, Robert.
  Protestant Church Music
    in America, 681
Stockhausen, Karlheinz, 646
  Zeitmasse, 218
Stockhausen: Life and Work,
  646
The Story of Rock, 747
Strauss, Johann.
  An der Schönen Blauen
    Donau, 87
  Die Fledermaus, 478
  Geschichte aus dem
    Wiener Wald, 88
  Kaiser-Walzer, orches-
    tra, 89
Strauss, Richard, 647
  Don Juan, 90
  Der Rosenkavalier, 479
  Salome, 480
  Songs. Selections, 421
  Till Eulenspiegels
    lustige Streiche, 91
Stravinsky: The Composer
  and His Works, 648
Stravinskiĭ, Igor' Fedoro-
  vich, 648

Stravinskiĭ (cont.)
  Concertino, string quar-
    tet, 148
  Double canon, string
    quartet, 285
  In memoriam Dylan Thomas,
    422
  Octet, winds, 242, 369
  L'oiseau feu. Suite, 92
  Petroushka, 93
  Pieces, string quartet,
    149, 286
  Poems, 423
  The Rake's Progress, 481
  Le sacre du printemps,
    94
  Septet, piano, winds &
    strings, 236
  Symphonie des Psaumes,
    527
Stuckenschmidt, H. H.
  Arnold Schoenberg: His
    Life, World and Work,
    640
Studies and Etudes for
  Timpani, 913
Studies and Melodious
  Etudes for Mallet, 919
Sullivan, Arthur Seymour,
  649
  H.M.S. Pinafore, 482
  Mikado, 483
  The pirates of Penzance,
    484
Summer Music, 329
A Survey of Musical Instru-
  ment Collections, 577
A Survey of Musical Instru-
  ments, 578
"Susanna," "Jeanie," and
  "The Old Folks at Home,"
  687
Suzuki in the String Class,
  944
Suzuki Piano School, 934
Suzuki, Shinichi.
  Sato Cello School, 829

Suzuki (cont.)
  Suzuki Piano School,
    934
  Suzuki Violin School,
    817
Suzuki Violin School, 817
Swan Lake, 32
Symphonie des Psaumes,
  527
Symphonie fantastique,
  20
Symphonic Metamorphosis of
  Themes by Weber, 52
Symphony of Psalms, 527

Tales from the Vienna
  Woods, 88
The Tales of Hoffmann,
  471
Taussig, Harry.
  Folk Style Autoharp,
    842
  Instrumental Techniques
    of American Folk
    Guitar, 836
  Teach Yourself Guitar,
    837
Tchaikovsky. See
  Chaĭkovskiĭ, Petr Il'ich
Tchaikovsky, 599
Teach Yourself Guitar, 837
Technic Treasury, 924
Technical Studies for the
  Violoncello, 827
Technical Studies for
  Treble Woodwind Instru-
  ments, 857
Telemann, Georg Philipp,
  650
Tempo, 811
Terry, Charles S.
  Bach: A Biography, 587
Thayer's Life of Beethoven,
  590
They All Played Ragtime,
  725
Thirty Etudes, 832

30 [Thirty] Etudes Speciales
  for Viola Solo, 822
35 [Thirty-five] Technical
  Studies for Alto and Bass
  Clarinet, 869
36 [Thirty-six] Studies
  (Elementary and Progres-
  sive) for Viola Solo, 820
36 [Thirty-six] Studies for
  Trombone with F Attach-
  ment, 905
Thirty-Three Concert
  Etudes, 878
This Business of Music,
  581
This Day, 528
Thompson Easiest Piano
  Course, 935
Thompson, John.
  Thompson Easiest Piano
    Course, 935
Thompson, Kenneth.
  A Dictionary of Twentieth
    Century Composers, 553
Thompson, Oscar.
  International Cyclopedia
    of Music and Musicians,
    534
Thomson, Virgil, 710
  American Music Since 1910,
    710
  Songs from William Blake,
    424
  Virgil Thomson, 711
Three Penny Opera, 498
Till Eulenspiegels lustige
  Streiche, 91
Timpani Student, 914
Tirro, Frank.
  Jazz: A History, 746
Tobey, Cliff.
  A Guide to Playing the
    Recorder, 884
Toll, Robert C.
  Blacking Up, 761
Tonadillas, 391
Tosca, 474

Traum, Happy.
  Flat-pick Country Guitar,
    838
La Traviata, 489
Treasury of American
  Song, 447
The Treasury of Scales
  for Band, 951
The Treasury of Scales
  for Orchestra, 947
Trevor, C. H.
  The Oxford Organ Method,
    942
Tristan und Isolde, 497
Il Trovatore, 490
Tustin, Whitney.
  Technical Studies for
    Treble Woodwind Instru-
    ments, 857
Twentieth-Century Composers,
  666
25 [Twenty-five] Studies in
  Scales and Chords for
  Bassoon, 874
Twenty-Four Etudes for the
  Flute, 848
Twenty-One Etudes for the
  Violoncello, 26
21 [Twenty-one] Foundation
  Studies for Alto and
  Bass Clarinet, 870
26 [Twenty-six] Etudes
  Brillantes for Viola
  Solo, 823
200 [Two Hundred] New
  Studies, 887
221 [Two Hundred Twenty-
  One] Progressive Studies
  for Trombone, 889
Two Poems and Three Japanese
  Lyrics, 423
Tyrell, H. W.
  Advanced Studies for B^b
    Bass, 911
  40 [Forty] Progressive
    Studies for the Trom-
    bone, 904

The Ugly Duckling, 406
United States Music, p. 95
Upton, William T.
  Anthony Philip Heinrich,
    695
Urban Blues, 729

Varèse: A Looking Glass
  Diary, 712
Varèse, Edgard, 651, 712
  Octandre, 243
Varèse, Louise.
  Varèse: A Looking Glass
    Diary, 712
Variations on a Theme by
  Haydn, 28
Variety Music Cavalcade
  1620-1969, 583, 756
Vaughan Williams, 652
Vaughan Williams, Ralph,
  652
  Mystical songs. Piano-
    vocal score, 425
  Songs of travel, 426
  This day, 528
Verdi, 654
Verdi: A Documentary
  Study, 653
Verdi, Giuseppe, 653-54
  Aida, 485
  Un ballo in maschera,
    486
  Otello, 487
  Requiem, 529
  Rigoletto, 488
  La Traviata, 489
  Il trovatore, 490
Verklärte Nacht, 79, 171,
  307
Le vilain petit canard, 406
Villa-Lobos, Heitor.
  Bachianas brasileiras,
    95, 427
Vincenzo Bellini: His Life
  and His Operas, 591
Vinton, John.
  Dictionary of Contemporary
    Music, 554

Violins and Violinists,
  660
Virgil Thomson, 710
The Virtuoso Pianist in
  60 Exercises, 930
Visits to St. Elizabeth's,
  412
Vivaldi, Antonio, 655
  Gloria, 530
Voices from the Mountains,
  718
Voxman, Himie.
  Introducing the Alto or
    Bass Clarinet, 871
  Rubank Advanced Method,
    Bassoon, 875
  Rubank Advanced Method,
    Clarinet, 864
  Rubank Advanced Method,
    Cornet or Trumpet,
    897
  Rubank Advanced Method,
    Eb or BBb Bass, 910
  Rubank Advanced Method,
    Flute, 853
  Rubank Advanced Method,
    French Horn, 890
  Rubank Advanced Method,
    Oboe, 859
  Rubank Advanced Method,
    Saxophone, 881
  Rubank Advanced Method,
    Trombone or Baritone,
    901
  Selected Studies for
    Flute, 852
  Selected Studies for
    Oboe, 858

Wachet auf, ruft uns die
  Stimme, 505
Wagner: A Documentary Study,
  656
Wagner as Man and Artist,
  657
Wagner, Richard, 656-57
  Gedichte von Mathilde
    Wesendonck, 428

Wagner (cont.)
  Gotterdämmerung, 493
  Lohengrin, 491
  Die Meistersinger von
    Nürnberg, 492
  Das Rheingold, 494
  Der Ring des Nibelungen,
    493-6
  Siegfried, 495
  Tristan und Isolde, 497
  Die Walküre, 496
Walker, Alan.
  Chopin Companion, 600
  Liszt, 619
  Robert Schumann: The Man
    and His Music, 643
Walker, Frank.
  Hugo Wolf: A Biography,
    659
Die Walküre, 496
Waller, Gilbert R.
  Waller Vibrato Method
    for Strings, 948
Waller Vibrato Method for
  Strings, 948
Warrack, John.
  Tchaikovsky, 599
Water Music, 46
Watson, Derek.
  Bruckner, 597
Weaver, William, ed.
  Verdi: A Documentary
    Study, 653
Weber, Fred.
  Alto Clarinet Student,
    866
  First Division Band
    Method, 952
Weber, Karl Maria Friedrich
  Ernst, Freiherr von.
  Der Freischutz. Overture,
    96
  Quintet, clarinet &
    strings, op. 34, Bb
    major, 352
Webern, Anton von, 658
  Bagatelles, string quar-
    tet, op. 9, 150, 287